Software Prototyping

Adoption, Practice and Management

M. F. Smith

McGRAW-HILL BOOK COMPANY

London · New York · St Louis · San Francisco · Auckland · Bogotá
Caracas · Hamburg · Lisbon · Madrid · Mexico · Milan · Montreal
New Dehli · Panama · Paris · San Juan · São Paulo · Singapore
Sydney · Tokyo · Toronto

Published by

McGRAW-HILL Book Company (UK) Limited

SHOPPENHANGERS ROAD · MAIDENHEAD · BERKSHIRE · ENGLAND

TEL: 0628-23432; FAX: 0628-770224

British Library Cataloguing in Publication Data
Smith, M. F. (Michael F.)
Software prototyping: adoption, practice and management.
1. Computer systems. Software. Development
I. Title
005.1

ISBN 0-07-707241-3

Library of Congress Cataloging-in-Publication Data
Smith, M. F. (Michael F.)
Software prototyping: adoption, practice, and management / M.F.
Smith.
p. cm.
Includes bibliographical references and index.
ISBN 0-07-707241-3
1. Computer software—Development. I. Title.
QA76.76.D47S58 1991
005. 1—dc20   90-36911

12345 PB 94321

Typeset by Book Ens Limited, Baldock, Herts.
and printed and bound in Great Britain by Billing & Sons Ltd, Worcester

To
Joan Smith

Contents

Acknowledgements   xi

1. Introduction   1

    1.1   The failure of computing   1
    1.2   Custom software   2
    1.3   Development approaches   3
    1.4   The prototyping approach   5
    1.5   Prototyping and travelling   5
    1.6   Managing the unmanageable   7
    1.7   Conclusion   8

Part One   Background to prototyping   11

2. Success, failure, and software development   13

    2.1   Success and failure   13
    2.2   Proof and dialectic   14
    2.3   Common computing successes   16
    2.4   Software failure   16
    2.5   The PC: a computing success story?   18
    2.6   PC success factors   20
    2.7   Is software a failure?   22
    2.8   Software success   23
    2.9   Discussion   24

3. People and computing   26

  3.1   Is software development creative?   26
  3.2   Programmers and analysts   27
  3.3   What do computers do to programmers?   28
  3.4   Where do programmers come from?   30
  3.5   Software managers   31
  3.6   Users   32
  3.7   Conclusion   33

4. Custom software   35

  4.1   Why produce custom software?   35
  4.2   Externally produced software   37
  4.3   Why does custom software fail?   38
  4.4   Discussion   41

5. Introduction to prototyping   42

  5.1   Definitions   43
  5.2   The basic prototype   45
  5.3   Prototyping strategies   45
  5.4   Scope of prototyping   47
  5.5   The reality of prototyping   48
  5.6   Discussion   49

Part Two   Rationale for prototyping   51

6. Prototyping benefits and problems   53

  6.1   Benefits of prototyping   55
  6.2   Prototyping problems   57
  6.3   Where to adopt prototyping   59
  6.4   What prototyping does not address   59
  6.5   Discussion   59

7. Prototyping and traditional software development   61

  7.1   The fatal flaws   63
  7.2   Prototyping in traditional development   65
  7.3   Conclusion   66

8. Prototyping and software engineering   68

  8.1   Productivity   69
  8.2   Quality   70
  8.3   Manageability   70

8.4   Methodologies   71
8.5   Problems in software engineering   73
8.6   Computer-aided software engineering   74
8.7   Formal methods   76
8.8   Conclusion   77

Part Three   Adoption of prototyping   79

9.   Strategies for adopting prototyping   81

9.1   Prototyping transfer   82
9.2   Preliminary evaluation   82
9.3   Management support   83
9.4   Technical issues   85
9.5   Prototyping tools and adoption   86
9.6   Conclusion   86

10.   Prototyping and people   87

10.1   Attitude   87
10.2   Prototyping and prototypers   88
10.3   Prototyping and software managers   90
10.4   Prototyping and users   91
10.5   Prototyping and non-computing management   92
10.6   Education   93
10.7   Conclusion   94

11.   Adoption: prototyping tools   95

11.1   Business effective prototyping tools   95
11.2   Cost   96
11.3   Functionality of prototyping tools   97
11.4   Rapid implementation of prototypes   97
11.5   Deliverability of prototypes   98
11.6   Maintainability of prototypes   99
11.7   Conclusion   100

Part Four   Prototyping management and practice   101

12.   Appropriate management styles for prototyping   103

12.1   The need for management change   104
12.2   Predicting development time and cost   104
12.3   Problems of time-driven management   106
12.4   Management by priority   107

12.5   Leadership and prototyping   109
12.6   Conclusion   110

13. Management issues in prototyping   112

13.1   The role of the software manager   112
13.2   The role of the prototyping manager   114
13.3   Friction between users and prototypers   114
13.4   Public exposure of success and failure   115
13.5   Knowing when to stop and when to keep going   116
13.6   Maintaining business relevance and validity   117
13.7   Maintaining technical quality and standards   118
13.8   Deliverables   119
13.9   Evaluating prototyping success   121
13.10 Conclusion   122

14. Structure of prototyping   123

14.1   Planning   123
14.2   Contracts and charging   125
14.3   Prototyping   126
14.4   Implementation with teams   128
14.5   Integration   129
14.6   Final evaluation   130
14.7   Delivering prototypes   132
14.8   The activities of delivery   133
14.9   Achieving delivery   133
14.10 Prototyping and databases   136
14.11 Discussion   138

15. Tools for prototyping   139

15.1   Conventional prototyping tools   139
15.2   Compiled high-level languages   140
15.3   Interpreted high-level languages   142
15.4   Tool sets   143
15.5   Database management systems   144
15.6   Hybrid solutions   146
15.7   Fourth-generation languages   147
15.8   Spreadsheets   147
15.9   Screen editors and word processors   148
15.10 Executable specifications   148
15.11 Object-oriented languages   149
15.12 Artificial intelligence languages and tools   150
15.13 Other conventional software tools   150
15.14 Conclusion   150

16. Prototyping and the human–computer interface   152

    16.1   Similar problem domains   152
    16.2   HCI problems   153
    16.3   Discussion   154

Part Five   Conclusion   157

    Prototyping and organizations   158
    Throw-away and evolutionary prototyping   158
    Recommendations   159
    Conclusion   160

Part Six   Case Studies   163

    1   Prototyping case I   165
    2   Prototyping case II   176

References   191

Index   198

Acknowledgements

I would like to thank the following people for their assistance with this book:

Mrs D. R. Graham
Professor C. A. R. Hoare
Dr Y. Hoffner
Professor D. Ince
Mr V. Iyer
Mr. J.-M. Lador
Mr D. Pointon
Colonel G. R. Smith
Mrs J. B. V. Smith
Miss K. W. Smith
Mr A. D. Ware
Dr B. T. Wells
Dr R. M. Yorston

I particularly would like to thank Mr David Whitehead of ISTEL Limited for supplying many references and for proofreading the manuscript several times.

Mike Smith

1
Introduction

It has almost become a cliché that computers are as essential to modern society as water and electricity. It may well be that we are in the midst of a revolution that has been caused by computers. This revolution may prove to have effects as great as those of the Industrial Revolution of the nineteenth century. The pressures on businesses and other organizations* to computerize in the hope of increasing efficiency or gaining competitive advantage are almost overwhelming (Porter and Millar, 1985).

As a result of wide-scale adoption, applications carried out by computers are becoming progressively more sophisticated. At the same time, the responsibilities assigned to computers are becoming more important. There are signs that computers are changing the fundamental ways in which most organizations operate. Computers are even enabling the full integration and interdependence of critical business functions between organizations. The economic and organizational consequences of de-computerization or even de-emphasis on computerization are almost inconceivable.

1.1 The failure of computing

The demand for new software appears to be greater than the capability to produce it (Boehm and Papaccio, 1988). In spite of the pervasiveness of computers, evidence of the failure of computing is extensive. The annual, world-wide cost of producing computer software may exceed $250 billion by 1990 (Boehm and Papaccio, 1988). As many as half of all software develop-

* Throughout the book, I will use the term 'organization' to mean businesses and other types of structured enterprises, including government. I will use expressions such as 'business software and business activity' in place of 'organizational software and organizational activity', however, since the latter has no commonly understood meaning.

1

ments may never reach operational status (Boar, 1984). Computing operations generally appear to be compared unfavourably with other parts of organizations (Jones, 1986) in terms of cost, growth, quality, and risk.

The major problems of computing are generally recognized to be in the production of software. The process of producing software is seen as being deficient in the following respects:

- Productivity.
- Quality and maintainability.
- Manageability.

Often, the deficiencies of software are so obvious that it can never be delivered. If delivered, software may suffer under-utilization or premature abandonment. Most software deficiencies do not stem from technical problems, but from not producing the software that users need and want (Boar, 1984).

The legendary success of computer hardware only throws the perceived failure into even sharper relief (IEEE, 1989). Over the past 20 years, computer hardware has been the focus of dramatic technological breakthroughs, a startling degree of manufacturing automation, and major business investment and interest. Hardware performance has doubled almost every year, development cycles have shortened, costs become lower, components become smaller, and reliability has improved radically (Bell *et al.*, 1978).

Over the past 20 years, software has become a major business activity. In contrast to hardware, however, software productivity is generally perceived to have shown only modest improvement. Manageability of software development has become no easier and quality appears to be little improved over this period. For example, a recent study (Shandle, 1989, p. 74) reveals that over 70 per cent of United States Department of Defense software contractors employ no better than an 'ad hoc or, possibly, chaotic process' for managing their software development projects.

1.2 Custom software

Organizations often produce software that is customized to meet their specialized business or operational requirements. Custom software can give organizations a 'competitive edge' in their use of computers by providing a unique function or enhanced efficiency. The main problem area in the production of software, however, is thought to be in the creation of custom software (Boehm, 1987). Custom software must, therefore, be considered an activity that carries a high risk of failure.

Typical problems of custom software are that it:

- Is expensive and difficult to develop.
- Has a 'stormy' introduction to its users.
- Does not satisfy the needs and expectations of users.

- Does not meet the needs of the business.
- Is expensive and difficult to maintain.

Custom software mainly consists of simple, repetitive processing of complex databases (Talbot and Witty, 1983). More often than not, there is a requirement for highly specialized and sophisticated, in the true sense of that word, interfaces between the custom software and its users. From a technical point of view, however, there are likely to be few problems encountered in producing most custom software. In spite of the unchallenging technical nature of custom software and easy access to users, development and introduction of custom software is likely to prove troublesome. Most of the trouble can be attributed to the software not meeting the wants and needs of its users.

Examine almost any organization in which custom software is being introduced. You probably will find a long history of unhappy users, unsatisfied business needs, unanticipated costs, unmet schedules, and poor quality. Look, too, at computing installations in which custom software is mature. Here, you are likely to find that software development staff spend so much time maintaining existing custom applications that they are unable to meet the demands for new ones. Any change of the existing software is likely to incur a substantial risk of causing more problems than benefits. This software has reached 'maintenance critical mass'. Many of the problems of maintenance are related to not having met the needs of the users in the first place. These are exacerbated by not being able to accommodate changing needs in the software during its lifetime.

In sites that produce custom software, it is not unusual to find that dozens of man-years of custom software have been abandoned (Jones, 1986). Some of the software may have been abandoned without ever having been used seriously. Abandonment usually is done without hesitation or serious attempt at salvage. It is worrying that the business benefits of computing, in general, have proven difficult to locate, quantify, and predict (King, 1983). The benefits of customized software are even more tenuous and difficult to identify, even where the need for custom software is genuine.

1.3   Development approaches

The deficiencies and risks of software development have been recognized for almost as long as there have been computers. Considerable effort has been expended over the past 30 years to devise means of improving the process of producing software and to avoid software development 'anarchy'. Two widely accepted approaches to software development have evolved:

- The traditional or analytical approach.
- The software engineering approach.

The traditional, analytical approach to software development is the older and more commonly used of the two. This approach generally has been seen to have been manifestly unsuccessful, both in the literature and in the experience of most computer professionals. The analytical approach is so deeply institutionalized in computing, however, that it continues to be employed almost universally. The problems of this traditional approach to software development are explored in Chapter 7.

The direct successor to the traditional, analytical approach to development is software engineering. The present trends in software engineering mainly appear to mechanize and make more rigorous the traditional approach to software development. There is, however, considerable emphasis on the need to employ special-purpose software 'tools' to practice software engineering. Although there has been much enthusiasm in the past 10 years for software engineering, there seems to be little convincing evidence that it is significantly more effective than the analytical approach. It is certain, though, that a great deal more investment is required. Software engineering is discussed in Chapter 8.

The analytical and the software engineering approaches are based on three shared assumptions. The first assumption is that all the requirements and needs of applications can be analysed and understood adequately by the users and software developers before development begins. Complete understanding, however, can rarely be achieved in a software development of any realistic size (Boar, 1984).

There also is an assumption in these two approaches that software needs and requirements will be stable throughout the development process. In fast-moving organizations or in protracted developments, however, requirements and needs almost certainly will change before the software is completed. Both approaches also fail to instil appreciation that the processes of software development and delivery are themselves almost certain to change the wants and needs of users (McCracken and Jackson, 1982).

Finally, there is an assumption in both the traditional, analytical approach and software engineering that users understand fully the technical documentation presented to them (Mason and Carey, 1983). These documents tend to be lengthy, technically arcane, and focus on the internal workings of the software. Yet the clients' approval is demanded as proof that their requirements have been accurately analysed. I believe that few clients read or understand these documents completely. Software engineering may only make this problem worse (Webster, 1988) by adding several layers of technical complexity and volume to the documentation.

For many developments, the base assumptions of the analytical and software engineering approaches are fallacious in part or in whole. Neither development approach makes adequate provision for error, incomplete understanding, uncertainty, or change. Thus, it should come as no great surprise that software developments often fail.

1.4 The prototyping approach

The prototyping of software is an approach to software development that appears to challenge many of the assumptions of traditional software development and software engineering practice. Recent interest in the subject of prototyping has been stimulated by various studies (Boehm *et al.*, 1984; Dearnley and Mayhew, 1984; Hekmatpour and Ince, 1986; Law, 1985; Nosek, 1984). These studies suggest considerable productivity and quality benefits from prototyping, even when conventional programming languages are used. The development of specialized prototyping tools (Budde *et al.*, 1984; Lugi and Ketabchi, 1988) has further stimulated interest in the subject.

The features of prototyping are the following:

* It depends on evolution of the software.
* There is no assumption of perfect knowledge of the application before implementation in prototyping.
* It directly involves end-users of the software during all stages of software development.
* Changes in user requirements and needs during development can be accommodated.

Prototyping has long been used by software developers to validate software functions on a small scale. Prototyping on a larger scale is far less common, however. In the more revolutionary form of prototyping — evolutionary prototyping — software is developed and delivered incrementally to the users. Requirements are added or deleted as the software evolves, continually and *in situ*, towards a satisfactory form.

Unlike the traditional and software engineering approaches, prototyping can be easy and inexpensive to adopt. There are those who consider special software tools essential to prototyping (Lugi, 1988). The essential feature of prototyping does not appear to be dependent on tools, however. It is the evolutionary mode of development and the direct involvement of users in the software development process that are essential to prototyping. Prototyping can be carried out successfully with software development tools already in use.

1.5 Prototyping and travelling

A reasonable analogy to the various styles of software development may be found in approaches to travel. The analytical software development approach seems much like the package tour. Here, the needs of travellers are assumed to be known totally in advance or it is understood that travellers will accept the limitations of the tour. As a result, every step of the trip can be planned. This permits transport and accommodation to be booked cheaply in advance. If anything goes seriously wrong, however, the trip may degenerate into a complete disaster. The travellers' needs and expectations may have changed during the trip. The trip itself may have altered the travellers' needs and expectations. Even if everything goes well, travellers may miss opportunities to improve their trip because changes are not permitted.

The software engineering approach, perhaps unkindly, seems analagous to the way one imagines an Intourist package tour to have been during the height of the Cold War. Here, everything is carefully planned in minute detail to ensure that what may be unknowable is thought to be known; or, at least, no one will admit any uncertainty. There are masses of complex paperwork, although a good deal of it is automated on the side of the producers. The travellers receive volumes of information, in Russian, about the intended tour. Once travelling, there are controls and guards to ensure that the plan is followed rigidly.

An analogy to the software anarchy approach might be the knapsack and hitch-hiking mode of travel. Here, the travellers just decide to go, have few cares and very low costs. They may have a very good time or they may have a very bad time. They cannot be sure of arriving at any exact destination or in any particular time, and hence this is not likely to be a mode of travel acceptable to the businessman or woman. In software, however, anarchy is more common than is generally admitted.

The travelling parallel to prototyping is that it is similar to the way in which experienced business travellers tend to travel. These travellers know where they are going and recognize that good planning is an essential mental exercise to getting there with a minimum amount of cost and fuss. They know, however, that trips rarely go exactly as planned. Baggage should be kept to a minimum and, if possible, carried with them. They know that travel requirements may change during the trip or as a result of their travels. They keep their options open as late as possible, buy open tickets, keep a flexible frame of mind, and inform the people they intend to visit of any changes in plan. They also accept that their trip may cost more than if they took a package tour or hitch-hiked.

Obviously, neither the package tour nor the hitch-hiking approach is suitable for the business traveller. In package tours, costs are low if everything goes to plan. If package tour travellers get lost, however, the tour goes on without them. If the tour does not go where the travellers were expecting to go, then they will have to pay for both the disappointing tour and the next one they think will get them where they want to go. Hitch-hiking is too uncertain for the business traveller to consider, except in an emergency.

It is possible to belabour the travelling analogy further to show the absurdity of users committing themselves to software development from documentation produced from traditional analysis. Imagine that our travellers are intending to spend a large sum of money on an aeroplane flight. The travel agent promptly pulls out engineering drawings of the aircraft, the preflight maintenance check-list, the pilot's flight plan, aeronautical navigation maps, and the like. Oh yes, the travel agent is only able to supply notional travel costs and dates.

It is exceedingly unlikely that anyone would attempt to make a decision about the flight from engineering drawings, nor would they be likely to contact that travel agent again. Yet, it is on a similar basis on which much software development routinely proceeds and on which large sums of money are committed. This is often because people are afraid to say, 'I don't know what you are talking about. I'm not a computer professional and I don't understand what you are telling me. I'll only know what it is that I wanted when you show me a working product.' To this demand, there seems to be only one possible positive answer: 'I'll create a prototype.'

1.6 Managing the unmanageable

This leads on to what is, perhaps, a contentious point about software development. It is instructive to ask what it is that software development approaches are really expected to deliver. It is my contention that these mainly offer management a comforting veneer of pseudo-control. In my experience, and this is confirmed in the literature (e.g. Boehm *et al.*, 1984 W. Myers, 1989), software development is heavily geared to human-related aspects. Human factors are notoriously unpredictable. As a result, software development simply may not be a highly predictable or easily managed process.

The story of the development of the highly successful Lotus 1-2-3 spreadsheet is illustrative (Hammonds, 1989). The first release of 1-2-3 was apparently produced by two or three programmers, working without management. The third release, however, involved 35 programmers, a large management team, and took three years to produce. The delivery of the third release of 1-2-3 was postponed three times and the company's share price declined by over 50 per cent as a result of this delay.

At the time of writing, it is uncertain if Lotus Development Corporation will ever recover its position in the marketplace. The reason this is a particularly significant story is that Lotus is a company that produces software and only software. It is a company that was said to have a strong, able, and smart management team (Nulty, 1989). If a company of this sort finds it difficult to manage its software development, what chance does an 'ordinary' company have of producing software successfully?

Stories such as the one about Lotus, a similar tale about Ashton-Tate's dBASE IV (Cole, 1989), and the widely perceived failure of custom software development should suggest that something is seriously wrong with the way in which software development is managed. Software management methods have become institutionalized. This is not because they are known to be effective. It appears more that it is in the interests and desires of software managers to appear to be in control, even if they are not. Other management in the organization is unable or unwilling to expose the weaknesses of its own software management.

The comforting veneer of management may be politically essential for effective operation, or even for survival, of software development operations within large companies. This veneer, however, has been slavishly imitated by smaller companies because it is 'the done thing'. Large companies may be able to afford the additional overhead, but smaller ones cannot.

There is a possibility that custom software development is inherently a craft, if not an art, activity in at least some of its parts. It therefore may not be an activity that can necessarily be profitably or efficiently converted into a predictable, mechanized activity. Prototyping can accommodate this view of software development; traditional approaches cannot.

1.7 Conclusion

As far as I can see, prototyping seems the most suitable software development approach for discovering and communicating the needs and requirements of users of custom software. There is a strong view beginning to appear in the technical computing literature confirming the benefits of the prototyping approach in general. From personal experience, I have been able to observe that prototyping of software is an approach that can result in dramatic improvements in custom software development.

Prototyping, in many organizations, may be able to improve significantly the effectiveness of custom software development and improve the quality of the software delivered. Inappropriate or uncontrolled use of prototyping, however, could prove detrimental to the quality, maintainability, or manageability of software. The ability to introduce and manage prototyping should be key to achieving success in delivering computing applications, particularly in small and medium-sized organizations.

My comments about prototyping are aimed largely at the internal computing operations of small and medium-sized organizations. Internal computing operations are supposed to produce customized software to meet the needs of their host organization. Typically, they are also supposed to deliver and support computing applications created outside the organization (i.e. packaged software). Internal computing is distinct from the segment of computing that produces packaged applications specifically for sale to other organizations. It is the internal computing operations in which much custom software is produced and in which software failure appears to be so prevalent.

A main theme of this book is exploring the value of prototyping for determining user needs and requirements in custom software development in small and medium-sized organizations. I have tried to contrast prototyping with conventional software development approaches, especially that of software engineering. Droll analogies, provocative statements, and opinions aside, I also have attempted to provide a useful background to and a general overview of prototyping.

The consequence of a favourable view on the value of prototyping may be its adoption within an organization. I have provided some advice about the partial or complete replacement of analytical or software engineering approaches by prototyping. I also present some common-sense suggestions about adopting, using, and keeping control of prototyping within conventional business environments. Perhaps more significantly, I propose that major changes in software development management style may be beneficial, or even essential, to the effective use of prototyping.

Part One
Background to prototyping

This section, 'Background to prototyping', may strike some readers as confusingly indirect or even completely irrelevant. They may say, 'This is supposed to be a book about prototyping. So when's this guy going to start beating the drum for it?' They may also say 'Look, my boss told me he wants us to start prototyping at nine o'clock on Monday. I haven't got time to read all this philosophical garbage!' It is my view, however, that most of the problems of software development are related to complex and subtle human factors. These factors are too often ignored by software developers. Prototyping may be even more sensitive to human factors than other development approaches. Addressing and understanding the apparently peripheral background subjects of this section are, I believe, as important as launching an immediate and direct attack in favour of prototyping.

Prototyping directly addresses many of the human factors that contribute to the problems of software development. Unfortunately, though, there is no pat, mechanistic formula for adopting, managing, and practising prototyping. Prototyping is more of an attitude, a 'way of life', or a philosophy for software development than a clearly defined methodology. Successful prototyping demands a deep appreciation of the complex human issues involved in software development. In a sense, the solution to the problems of software development already lies, literally, within our own hands, minds, and hard work.

Unlike some authors, I cannot foresee any stunning, universally applicable technological breakthroughs for software development. Those looking for a fresh and original approach are likely to be disappointed by this book. Prototyping is not a fresh subject. Prototyping may well be software development's oldest approach. It is an approach that is already well known and widely practised, even if it is not always recognized or admitted. Originality

is not particularly needed in this subject area, either. What is needed,
though, is a coherent rationale and an outline of practice for prototyping in
routine commercial software development. That is what I have set out to
achieve in this book.

2
Success, failure, and software development

Much of this book is concerned with success and failure. Most of us recognize that there is too much failure in software development. It is important, therefore, that the terms 'success' and 'failure' are defined carefully. The factors that create success or failure, either perceived or real, must be understood in the context of approaches to developing software. Only by understanding these factors can success in software development be achieved and failure avoided.

2.1 Success and failure

Success and failure are qualities that are both transient and difficult to quantify. According to the *Concise Oxford Dictionary* (Sykes, 1976), success is 'favourable outcome, accomplishment of what was aimed at; attainment of wealth or fame or position'. Failure is 'lack of success'.

Long-term survival may be the best indicator of success for an organization. There are other generally accepted and shorter-term indicators of organizational success:

- Profit.
- Planned growth.
- Satisfaction of customers and staff.
- Meeting of objectives.

Longevity may be as reliable an indicator of success for software (Kopetz, 1979) as it is for organizations. Users may grumble about even the best software, but genuinely useless or low-quality software rarely remains in use for long. Old software must have something in its favour if it continues to be used. This leads to the question of 'How old is old?' The answer, of course, is relative. Typically, however, software that is at least three years old can be considered old, although it is not uncommon to encounter software that is over 10 years old.

Success for software may be indicated, in the short term by the following:

- Demonstrable benefit to the organization.
- Continued use and enhancement.
- User satisfaction.
- Delivery to requirement, time, and budget.

For software to achieve longevity and success, it is likely that all of the indicators must be achieved to some degree or another. The indicators are also somewhat interdependent. For example, software that gives superb user satisfaction and high organizational benefit may be forgiven for being somewhat over its budget and for being a bit behind its delivery schedule. If, on the other hand, the software is very late and way over budget, it is unlikely to be perceived as successful, no matter how well it satisfies the other indicators.

— What kind of proof is there that prototyping is the best development approach?

2.2 Proof and dialectic

Central to the idea of succes and failure is proof. Proof is required to show that something has produced benefit, has been used, has given satisfaction, or has been delivered on time. Typically, proof is given in terms of measured performance. For example, typical proofs are that 'profits were up 47 per cent on last year' or 'nine out of ten owners expressed a preference for our product over theirs'. Measurement, therefore, is an essential part of proof (Jones, 1986).

In most areas of science, experimental proof is considered essential to demonstrate that something is true. The basis of scientific proof consists of the following:

- Measurement and comparison.
- Control experiments to show what would have happened if nothing had been done.
- Undertaking a sufficient number of experiments to demonstrate that the results are statistically significant.
- The reproducibility of experimental results by other researchers.

Other branches of science (e.g. geology and astronomy) are unable to prove the truth of their theories through experimental evidence. Here, generally accepted facts, produced by long and careful observation, are used as evidence to support theories.

Compared to the traditional sciences, investigation of software development approaches appears to fall short in providing acceptable scientific proof. The problem of assessing the impact of any software development approach, including prototyping, seems to be one of lack of controlled measurement, experimentation, and observation. In general, I tend to be pessimistic that unequivocal proof can be produced. This is because of the apparent near-impossibility of producing convincing experimental evidence (Raghaven and Chand, 1989) about software.

Lack of measurement appears to be a particular weakness (Boehm, 1987; Jones, 1986) of providing evidence about software approaches. Gilb (1976) states that there are theoretically and economically feasible ways in which all important software concepts can be measured. This may well be the case, but few software development projects are actually instrumented in such a way as to supply any convincing measurements, other than that of cost. At best, it may be possible only to provide more-or-less convincing inferences of comparative benefits between one development and a similar one. This, however, is far from being a proper experimental approach.

Statistically valid populations and controlled experiments are required as a part of scientific proof. Valid software experiments would be difficult and exceedingly expensive (Jones, 1986), however, if carried out on 'real' projects in computing. There are some examples of careful experimentation technique in computing (e.g. Scanlon, 1989), but much of the 'proof' available consists of anecdotes about the perceived success of using a technique in a single instance and without proper control. Even the study of Boehm *et al.* (1984) in favour of prototyping is weakened — a fact recognised by the authors — by having been carried out on a population of only seven programming teams, composed of students. This experiment, in common with most computer science studies, also neglects the Hawthorne Effect (Weinberg, 1971) in which the productivity of those being observed improves just because they are being observed.

Another problem is that most of the efforts to obtain proof of the benefits of software development approaches are conducted within large organizations, particularly within the defence and aerospace industries. The other major source of evidence comes from within the computing industry. These organizations carry out very large software development projects, often of a highly challenging technical nature, and with large budgets. I am sceptical of the direct relevance of much of this evidence to small and medium-sized organizations producing routine, custom business software with comparatively modest budgets.

Given that rigorous proof may be unlikely in computing studies (Jones, 1986), one is left mainly with dialectical (King and Kraemer, 1984) or 'argument' approaches (Perelman and Olbrechts-Tyteca, 1969) towards proof. Dialectic is 'investigating the proof of opinions . . . logical disputation' (Sykes, 1976). Two routes in dialectical investigation seem appropriate to the study of software development approaches. The first is to eleminate sources of evidence that are obviously self-interested or implausible, but to accept the remaining evidence as being valid to at least some degree. The second route is to attempt to demonstrate where approaches may be illogical, unsuccessful, risky, or otherwise flawed.

Dialecticism admittedly is a pretty poor alternative to rigorous measurement, experimental results, or large-scale observation. It appears to be the best technique available within the subject, however. At least, it should help verify that 'belief is kept conformable to fact' (Perelman and Olbrechts-Tyteca, 1969). I will apply this dialectical approach when discussing the merits of prototyping over the traditional software engineering approaches.

2.3   Common computing successes

One of the earliest commercial computing applications was for bookkeeping, payrolls, and billing (Nolan, 1979; King, 1983). Almost all large and medium-sized organizations have employed computerized finance systems for many years. Many small businesses now have their bookkeeping based on personal computers (PCs). Generally, these systems are stable, reliable, and long lived. Few companies could remain in business for long without their internal financial systems. In other words, the software that carries out this application appears to be successful.

Most companies rely on computers to a high degree in their personnel and administrative functions. Typical functions are employee administration, wages and payroll, performance review, and reporting for governmental purposes. Problems in this area of computing would be highly disruptive to most organizations. Again, these systems and their software can be seen, as a rule, to have been successful.

Word processors are essential to most organizations (Galitz, 1980) for routine preparation of correspondence and reports. Software is a critical component of word processing systems. More complex office automation systems have become increasingly important. Office automation includes the word processing function but also extends to management reporting, decision support, electronic publishing, time management, address lists, electronic mail, and some traditional data processing roles (Hirschheim, 1985). Generally, this area of computer application is perceived by users as being successful.

2.4   Software failure

Software may be very complex in its function and interrelation with people and organizations. There are many points at which software can go wrong, and in order to improve the success of software development it is important to know and understand these points of difficulty. A brief outline of some of the points of difficulty that are encountered in all types of software development follows.

Software often operates within a far wider context than its developers appreciate (Bessant and Dickson, 1982). Failure to appreciate and plan within this wider context of operation is a common cause of software failure. The following are some typical problems:

- Failure to understand total needs and requirements.
- Failure to foresee social impact (Rzevski, 1984).
- Unanticipated adverse impact on organization and people.
- Unrealistic expectations of benefits and rates of return.
- Unrealistic expectation of function.

Poor management can cause or contribute to software failure (Boehm, 1987). Management problems include the following:

- Insufficient financial and personnel resources allocated.
- Insufficient or inadequate skills, education, and training.
- Insufficient time allowed for development.
- Inadequate communication and reporting.
- Lack of control over external suppliers.

Poor design (Kopetz, 1979) of software is a point for potential failure. The following are typical design flaws:

- System not defined clearly or completely.
- Incorrect interpretation of the specification.
- Software proves technically infeasible.
- Neglect of special cases.
- Inadequate error handling.
- Final software runs too slowly.
- Size of the final software is too large for the hardware to be employed.
- Lack of appreciation of the interaction between the software solution and the problem to be solved.

Errors in implementation at a detail level can sap the vitality of software development and contribute to failure. Common errors (Kopetz, 1976) include the following:

- Incorrect syntax.
- Improper initialization of variables.
- Out of sequence or missing parameters in subroutine calls.
- Incorrect logic and branching.
- Misspelled variables.
- Variable type violations.
- Inadequate array sizes.
- Compiler error or misinterpretation.
- Operating system error or misinterpretation.

The success of good software can be compromised during its delivery and commissioning. In traditional software development, some aspects may not be determined until delivery. The following are some typical problems with delivery and commissioning:

- Lack of adequate consultation of users and management.
- Hostile users and management.
- Integration with existing systems proves impossible.
- Defective hardware.
- Erroneous data.

Once developed and delivered, software still can fail. Failure during operation can be caused by the following:

- Poor or inept maintenance.
- Poor, inept, untrained, or untrainable users.
- Support costs prove too high.
- Defective hardware.
- Erroneous data.
- Changed business requirements.

These are just a sample of some of the problems that can bedevil software. I am more often inclined to be surprised that software works at all than that it occasionally does not work. Prototyping developments can be affected by any of these problems but only addresses some of them. Consequently, prototyping alone cannot ensure success in software development.

2.5   The PC: a computing success story?

Before continuing to discuss the supposed major failure of computing, custom software, it may be instructive to discuss what is normally seen as one of computing's big successes: the personal computer. I think it would be generally accepted that PCs used in business are perceived as successes by their users (Lockett, 1986). Certainly, PC computing is almost the total antithesis of traditional custom computing.

To be fair, however, the supposed success of the PC should be measured by considering some of the criteria of success proposed earlier for computing applications in general, namely:

- Demonstrable benefit to the organization.
- Longevity; continued use of the application.
- User satisfaction with the application.
- Delivery of applications on time and to budget.

From a business point of view, I am sceptical that many PCs are successful in delivering demonstrable financial benefit. The amount of support required by PCs can be formidable, in relation to the actual amount of useful work they produce.

For example, not so long ago I took delivery of a new PC from a well-known manufacturer, operating primarily in the consumer marketplace. It took me about 10 hours to order the PC from a large supplier and to follow up missing components. It took me another 25 hours to get the PC running, the operating system installed, the printer interfaced to the new software, old software transferred, the PC sited, and to familiarize myself with new aspects of the system. In the first 100 hours of operation after installation, I spent at least another 15 hours doing back-ups, installing additional software, converting to new features, and backing out of new features.

Even if the average user takes no longer than I did to have a new PC up and running, 100 hours may be about as long as many users employ their PCs in a year. I would suggest that 50 hours of annual maintenance of PCs by their users is on the low side. Typical users also require a considerable amount of training and familiarization for their applications software as well (Lockett, 1986).These expenditures, however, normally are simply overlooked and continue to accumulate, year after year. As King (1983, p. 334) says, 'in very few cases does a computing installation, centralized or decentralized, get smaller and cheaper over time'. Another interesting question is how much of the time spent in PC applications is genuinely productive. For example, how much time is spent with users making documents attractive, when a merely routine appearance would be sufficient?

If longevity is considered on a hardware basis, then PCs could be considered spectacularly unsuccessful. In my experience, most PCs fall into disuse or are replaced by 'bigger and brighter' PCs within three years of purchase. For example, the original IBM PC of *circa* 1983 is no longer sold; one would have trouble giving them away. When was the last time you saw an original IBM PC working on someone's desk? Do you remember those Apple IIs, the Commodore Pets, and CP/M systems? What happened to those PCs? What happened to all their software, diskettes, and peripherals?

User satisfaction with PC software is legendary; I have rarely heard PC users complain about their software. However, I persistently find much PC software awkward to use, of low functionality, complicated, and of poor performance. In my present PC installation, I have been unable to get my brand-name word processor to interface fully with my supposedly supported, well-known laser printer. This PC word processor has been highly successful in terms of market penetration. I do not, however, consider it nearly as productive for 'serious' word processing as the UNIX editor vi and text formatter troff. Most users, fortunately, never have to get to the serious user stage.

Most PCs and their software are off-the-shelf items. Consequently, applications can be operational in days, if not hours. This is true as long as the application is one for which the software was specifically intended. I have seen cases where only modestly ambitious PC applications and installations have gone badly wrong. In these cases, delivery has stretched from days to months or installation has been aborted. In the long term, the PC application may not prove capable of handling the full-scale, operational application. Ask yourself, 'How many PC installations do you know of that are genuinely successful, from a business point of view? Of those, how many are not word processing or spreadsheet applications?' The chances are that you will not know of many.

The point of this discussion is that in the cold light of day PCs do not appear to be markedly more successful than typical custom software applications. The enthusiasm of PC users may just be a consequence of normal computer adoption patterns (King and Kraemer, 1984; Nolan, 1979). What PCs are good at, however, is giving users immediate results and strong gratification during the first few moments of use. This seems to leave a lasting aura of satisfaction, no matter how useless the product proves to be in serious use. Custom software developers and prototypers should take heed of this effect.

2.6   PC success factors

The perceived success of the PC shows that there is no inherent prejudice against the perception of success in computing activities in general. Emulating the factors that contribute to the perception of success in PCs may contribute to perception of success in other software developments. The following are some of the factors that I believe lead to the perception of success for PCs:

- Feelings of ownership and control.
- Immediate user gratification and enjoyment.
- Focused and discrete applications.
- New applications.
- Ease of abandonment.
- Low expectations.
- Little contact with computing professionals.
- They appear less expensive than they actually are.

Initially, most PCs were purchased by enthusiastic users, not imposed upon them by professional computing staff. It is natural, then, that these PC users feel that they own their computers and are in control of their computing facility. Even today where PCs have become part of computing operations, the PC activity tends to be heavily user driven in the selection and provision of hardware and software. At the level of the individual user, PCs tend to be used by one or two people who have genuine feelings of proprietorship about their PC. Because the PC is theirs, anything it does is seen as successful.

Initial impressions about success are lasting. PC software tends to provide immediate gratification and enjoyment for users. Most products are easy to use and valuable results often can be achieved within seconds of starting to use a product, even by total beginners. Often, the user interface is 'intuitively right'. This reduces frustration and provides a large amount of positive feedback. Users with a genuine application are likely to find using PCs a highly pleasurable experience. The value of games, demonstration programs, and other apparently time-wasting features for eliciting a favourable impression in users should not be underrated.

Many PC applications, such as word processors and spreadsheets, are focused and discrete. There is little expectation for them to be compatible with existing or future computer systems within the host organization. PC applications may not even be expected to be compatible with other PC products. The relative simplicity of PC applications may be a strong factor of success since this reduces the user burden of learning (Boehm, 1987) and improves reliability.

Applications provided by PCs tend to be new ones to their users. Because of this, user expectations about presentation, function, and performance are formed totally by the experience with PCs. As a result, there is no resistance from previously formed habits or expectations. For example, spreadsheets were introduced with PCs and there was nothing with which they could be compared unfavourably, except hand tabulation. Their functions and user interfaces have become more or less institutionalized so that all spreadsheets now appear similar in their appearance and operation.

PCs and their software initially tended to be purchased by users, rather than as a part of any organizational programme. As a result, PC hardware and software could be abandoned quietly and without adverse consequences to the purchasers. Successful PC users tend to make a lot of noise about their success; unsuccessful users tend to keep quiet and conceal their mistakes. It is instructive to snoop around PC user installations; you are likely to find a large investment in abandoned software, hardware, and supplies. There may even be totally unused earlier generations of PCs gathering dust or 'evaporating' to homes and schools. The ease of abandonment seems to enhance feelings of success by reducing the fear of failure.

Exceeding expectations normally arouses feelings of success. Users seem to have low expectations about what can be gained from using PCs. The small physical size and low purchase cost of PCs seems to cause an automatic down-scaling of expectations. Often there is an immediate 'poor little thing' reaction from even the most technophobic users. Users do not have particularly high expectations about their software either. They understand that 'what you've bought is what you've got'. Thus, they adapt their working habits to the software, rather than vice versa.

Another reason for the success of PCs may be that users are not forced into contact with computing professionals. PCs tend to be sold like office equipment, by salesmen with no greater technical knowledge of computing than the buyer. There is normally no involvement of computer professionals in the installation of software. It is my contention, developed later, that computer professionals themselves are one of the major sources of computing application failure.

Another reason for the perceived success of PCs may be that they appear to be far less expensive than they actually are. A modest capital investment for a PC, however, normally triggers an equal amount of expenditure for software, maintenance contracts, printers, diskettes, and accessories. Examine any one of the many catalogues available for PC supplies: you will see the most amazing range of plastic covers, screen glare reducers, special trollies, and the like. I can only assume that these items sell well enough to support a sub-industry. Few users probably ever bother to add up their total expenditure on their PC. They might get a shock if they did. The high cost should not be surprising, however: there is considerable evidence (King 1983) that decentralized computing is more expensive than centralized computing.

My experience is that PCs are not more demonstrably successful nor are they in reality less expensive than the general run of custom applications. They may even be less successful, from a business point of view (King, 1983). Nevertheless, the strong impression of success remains firmly planted in most people's minds. It is important that software developers, especially prototypers, understand why it is that PCs please, where so often their own software does not.

2.7   Is software a failure?

The progress of computer hardware in the last 40 years can be made to sound almost astounding. Comparisons made between the earliest computers and modern microprocessors can arrive at conclusions such as 'If the aviation industry had made similar progress . . . you could now fly around the world for about two cents . . . the trip would take about 80 seconds' (Arthur Andersen & Co., 1986). Although perhaps an exaggeration, there is considerable validity in this sort of comparison. This quantifiable and easily grasped progress lends an aura of success to the rapid progress in the field of hardware. Comparisons of hardware and software are generally uncomplimentary to software (IEEE, 1989).

It is instructive, however, to examine a computing textbook of 25 years ago (e.g. Hollingdale and Tootill, 1965) in the light of my definitions of success and failure. A significant part of the textbook is likely to be concerned with analogue computers. This is a major hardware technology which has disappeared from commercial computing (although poised to make a comeback as neural networks). Many other major items of hardware from that era are obsolete as well: magnetic drums, magnetic core, delay lines, cards, and paper tape. Where is this hardware of yesteryear? It is on the scrap-heap, of course. It has not survived.

On the other hand, much of the key software of 25 years ago is still recognizable today: ALGOL, FORTRAN, and COBOL. Many innovations have been made in software since then, too: higher-level languages, database management systems, packaged software, and improved user interfaces. Software productivity has increased dramatically in many aspects. For example, it is now possible to program a database application in an hour that might take several months to program in a third-generation language such as FORTRAN. I believe that the progress of software has probably been seriously underrated (Boar, 1984; Boehm, 1987).

Are we really just using the out-of-date software tools of long ago? Is it not possible instead that those software tools were actually well ahead of the hardware at the time? Is it possible that software progress simply is more difficult to quantify than hardware? No matter what the answers, my measure of success is longevity. Much software is very long lived and, therefore, it is successful. What this is intended to show is that there is no inherent quality in software that makes it prone to failure. The main failure of software may be simply that is it not perceived to be successful. Prototyping may offer a means to alter perceptions about software for the better.

2.8   Software success

It seems generally assumed that software has been less successful than hardware. Much of the software used today, however, or at least parts of it, is considerably older than the hardware on which it operates. For example, some compilers are 25 years old, most operating systems are at least 15 years old, and many applications (even PC applications) are over 10 years old. This suggests to me that some software has been outstandingly successful in having survived for so long. Nevertheless, there seems to be little question that software is generally perceived as a failure and a problem by non-technical users and managers (IEEE, 1989; Jones, 1986).

In my experience, the instances of perceived success in software are found most often in the following areas:

- Mature software in which virtually all errors have been found and eliminated or to which the users have become accustomed over time.
- Software of computers embedded into products (e.g. microprocessor engine management systems, household appliances).
- Packaged software emanating from software suppliers and acquired by users.

The reasons for the perceived success of mature software seem obvious.

Software that has survived the test of time either does some useful function well or has in some other way become institutionalized. Programmers have had sufficient time to work out the most obvious problems in mature software so that the software is relatively error free. Finally, the users, at least, have become familiar with the software and, at best, come to have a proprietorial attitude about it.

The reasons for the feelings of relative success about embedded and packaged software are less obvious than those for mature software. Embedded or packaged software may be of low quality, ill suited to the purposes intended, perform poorly, and be rife with errors. Many of these deficiencies are never rectified. Nevertheless, if the software survives delivery, the shortcomings tend to become accepted and overcome by users who then employ it as successfully as possible. This acceptance by users probably stems from the knowledge that there simply may be no way to improve the software.

It may seem cynical, but one common factor between mature software, embedded software, and packaged software appears to be that users are unlikely to have much, if any, contact with the computing technologists who wrote the software. The answer to the perception of success in software may be as much in the quality of the interaction between computing technologists and users as in the quality and function of the deliverables themselves.

Compared with normal expectations about human artefacts such as houses, software does not appear to be of abnormally low quality or function. The software industry appears to be more advanced in its ideas about quality then the building trade and software users more critical of flaws than house owners. The overall quality of the three new houses I have purchased in the last five years has appeared surprisingly low. Rectification, even of major faults, has been a long, tedious, and unstructured process. The idea of cosmetic quality (i.e. the 'human–house interface') appears to be almost totally lacking. Structural quality is something owners probably do not even want to think about.

Owners seem to accept the idea that the quality of houses should be relatively low because the buildings are handcrafted under difficult conditions. The expectations of purchasers appear to be surprisingly low for such a high-value, low-complexity, and frequently used item as a house. Yet, most people appear to be fairly well satisfied with their houses, and those engaged in the industry seem to make a lot of money building houses of indifferent quality. There may be a message here for custom software developers, namely that function and quality are not as important as meeting the basic wants and needs of the users.

2.9   Discussion

Software may be free from technical errors and still prove to be useless or even detrimental to organizations that use it. On the other hand, inadequate software may be able to give value and satisfaction if it fulfils the basic needs of its users. These needs may not always be for straightforward function either. This book is primarily concerned with avoiding the type of software failure that comes from producing software which does not meet the needs of its intended users. Prototyping offers an effective solution to this type of problem.

It seems widely accepted that organizations capable of responding rapidly to change are likely to succeed better (i.e. survive longer) than those that cannot. It also is believed that the pace of change in the business world is now noticeably more rapid than it has been in the past. Computer systems have become essential parts of most organizations. Consequently, it is imperative that the speed of software development is at least able to track the pace of change within the host organization. If the computer operation becomes a retarding influence, as is often the case, then the viability of the organization may be compromised. Then, the computer operation, quite rightly, can be judged a failure.

For small and medium-sized organizations, the ability to respond to change more rapidly than larger organizations may be an important component of their competitive success. It is exceedingly important, therefore, that computer operations within this size of organization do everything they can to ensure that they produce applications rapidly, avoid 'maintenance critical mass', and meet the needs of users and the business. It is my view that prototyping is an approach that is particularly appropriate for helping achieve these goals. Prototyping can contribute significantly to the success of organizations that use it effectively.

3
People and computing

The human element is often ignored in computing (Weinberg, 1971). Nevertheless, it remains one of the main sources of all computing problems, particularly the development of software. Every activity in computing ultimately relies on people. The availability of people, of any degree of competence, is a persistant problem in computing. People, not computers, are the most important component of computing; they also are its most fragile component.

Boehm (1981, 1987) suggests that the quality of staff is the most important part of software development by nearly half an order of magnitude. My feeling is that this is a significant underestimation, especially if the multiplicative effects of management quality are considered as well. I suspect that even among experienced programmers, differences in ability and experience can result in productivity and quality varying by as much as a factor of 10. Even then, individual performance may vary greatly with circumstances as vague as work environment, interest in the application, instantaneous motivation, and mood. Jones (1986) states that software productivity can vary from 200 lines per man-year to 30 000 lines per man-year in large organizations. Jones says, however, that changes in technology are only likely to affect software productivity by a factor of three. It seems logical to suspect that human quality may account for the remaining variability. Factors that might increase productivity 50-fold should be well worth considering.

3.1 Is software development creative?

In relation to many of the problems of software development approaches, there seems to be a central question, although one that is not often considered: is the development of software a creative activity or not? The *Concise*

Oxford Dictionary (Sykes, 1976) defines creative as 'showing imagination as well as routine skill'. Imagination (Sykes, 1976) is 'forming images or concepts of external objects not present to the senses'. These definitions almost precisely describe many of the key activities of software development.

I would be surprised if many people denied the notion that most software has some element of imagination (Heckel, 1984) in it. For example, the expression 'creating software' is used as often as 'producing software'. I have never heard anyone object to this usage. Computing people, however, generally prefer to think of themselves as engineers, scientists, and business people. In common with practitioners in those fields, they may resent artistic implications being made about their work (Snow, 1964). Those engaged in computing as a business may particularly dislike any notion that computing may be a creative and, therefore, an inherently unmanageable activity. Nevertheless, few would deny that there is an indispensable imaginative, and therefore creative, element to their work.

If, as I believe, there is a substantial amount of creativity required in programming, then what are the implications? One implication is that at least part of the software development process is not capable of being reduced to mechanical principles nor is it entirely predictable. Organizations should therefore consider seriously how much creativity should be permitted in their software, where it should be allowed, and how it should be contained. The first step, however, is accepting that developing software depends, to some extent, on creativity.

Creativity *per se* is not a problem in software development, except that it introduced an element of unpredictability into management. The problems stem more from poor documentation of creative output, total reliance on intuition, and unguided creativity. Make no mistake about creativity; it is not a bad thing. Gourmet restaurants, orchestras, and other supposedly creative activities derive only part of their 'competitive edge' through creativity. Without skill, discipline, practice, and sheer hard work, creativity has no great value.

3.2 Programmers and analysts

Many of the people engaged in software development may not be able to program, just as all those engaged in the entertainment industry are not necessarily entertaining. Programmers are the people who actually write or create software. They tend to stamp the industry strongly with their personalities. But be warned: for some reason the word 'programmer' is not particularly fashionable in the computer science field. Nevertheless, it is a descriptive, fairly accurate, and useful term.

Analysts are the designers of software. Many programmers become analysts and many analysts combine both roles. Most of the personal observations about programmers apply equally to analysts. Analysts have less direct contact with computers and more contact with other people. Consequently, they tend to have less marked personality traits than programmers. For brevity's sake, however, I will use the term programmer to mean analyst and programmer.

What Lord Snow (1964, p.7) said about scientists, 'inclined to be impatient to see if something can be done: and inclined to think that it can be done . . . tough and good and determined to fight it out', is generally true about programmers too. Not surprisingly, programming tends to attract people of reasonably high intelligence (Weinberg, 1971), who probably have some love of order and structure. Their love of order tends to be restricted to ordering the inanimate or imposing order externally. Curiously, most programmers have strong democratic tendencies, often bordering on the anarchic. Order imposed upon them by other people is likely to be resisted stoutly. Ironically, the structure and order of computers must be accepted whole-heartedly and totally to succeed in programming. Other characteristics typically associated with programmers are 'low social need and . . . high growth need' (Couger and Zawacki, 1980).

3.3   What do computers do to programmers?

Computing really is something fundamentally different: there is no other activity quite like it. The enthusiasm and energy that goes into the computing industry is at times almost amazing. Kidder's *The Soul of a New Machine* (1981), although about hardware, gives one of the best flavours of what computing can be like. Given the rapid technical development and immediate commercial applicability of computing, it is hardly surprising that the fundamental nature of computing is rarely discussed or questioned. Computer people are just too busy doing computing to have time to think very much about it as well. I almost feel the need to apologize for delving into the metaphysical treatment of such a practical, dynamic, and 'scientific' subject.

Programming is an intellectually difficult and challenging activity. The rules cannot be 'flexed' or arbitrated, as is so often the case in other human activities. The programmer must adhere totally to the logic of programming and meet the computer entirely on its own terms. This requires a major change in perception and style of thinking. For many people, this is a difficult mental change, but it is one that good programmers must be able to make. Given that many programmers spend substantially more waking time programming than engaged in any other activity, it is hardly surprising that their personalities are affected profoundly by it.

Whether programming is a creative activity or not, it does have a consistent, harmonious set of logical rules. These rules offer an almost infinite range of possibilities within an alien, but demonstrable, reality. Programming is a mentally challenging activity and one that provides continual, powerful feedback and immediate reinforcement (Loftus and Loftus, 1983).

It gives a constant feeling of achievement and even of power. Programming is emotionally 'clean' in that it is useful, profitable, and creative, and that no one is humiliated or hurt by the activity. Programming can be one of the most pleasurable, absorbing, and entertaining (King, 1983) of all activities.

It is largely irrelevant whether programming computers changes people or whether programming tends to attract certain types of personality. Programming is a challenging field with its own incontestable rules. Only those people fit for it, intellectually and emotionally, or able to change themselves, are likely to succeed. Programming is a rigorous filter for personalities; it is hardly surprising that a certain type of person tends to fall out at the bottom.

Can programming be harmful to one's mental health? The psychologists Loftus and Loftus (1983) provide several general behavioural indicators of psychological health:

1. Is the behaviour good for the person, in the sense of seeking rewards which do not harm others?
2. Is the person in touch with reality?
3. Is the person's behaviour markedly different from that of other people?

It is interesting to discuss some of the qualities that contribute to success in computing with these indicators of psychological health. Some of the qualities that lead to success in computing are the following:

- Clear, logical thinking, the ability to produce simple solutions, and an analytical turn of mind are essential to programming success. Programmers often come to attempt to apply computer-style logic to their human life, and this is frequently interpreted by others as arrogance, coldness, or unreality on their part.
- Persistence usually pays off in programming. There almost always is some way to do anything in computing, given enough persistence. This is a valuable quality in all walks of life, but if persistence spills over too much into everyday life, it may be interpreted as doggedness, aggressiveness, or cockiness.
- Willingness to experiment and change. In programming, there are rarely adverse or irrecoverable consequences to the actions taken. Experimentation, mutability, change, and malleability are essential parts of computing. Outside of computing, the consequences of change and experimentation may be expensive, time consuming, adverse, or unwelcome. Any change and experimentation are generally not welcomed. Excessive desire to change and experiment may be seen by others as being out of touch with reality, disloyal, unable to concentrate, or 'unsound'.
- High internal motivation (Couger and Zawacki, 1980). Programming provides much of its own motivation, reinforcement, and enjoyment. Good programmers tend to earn good salaries and are highly employable because of their skill. However, this generally makes them

unsympathetic to and out of touch with the normal pressures, boredom, and fears of the 'reality' of other people.

• Self-containment. Good programming tends to be a solitary and highly focussed activity that requires intense concentration but little interpersonal communication skill (Couger and Zawacki, 1980). This can lead to programmers working at odd hours and becoming distant, isolated, or cut off from other people. Programmers do communicate with each other (Weinberg, 1971) but the subject matter tends to be oriented towards computing.

The personal qualities that contribute to success in programming are, in themselves, similar to those that lead to success in other fields. In other human activities, a 'little of anything goes a long way', however, when it comes to exaggerated personality traits. Taken to extremes, these otherwise admirable behavioural traits can be seen, in the terms of Loftus and Loftus (1983), to be bordering on the psychologically unhealthy.

Computers are immune to poor personality traits: you don't have to be a politician to be a programmer. In general, the more extreme those traits conducive to good programming, however anti-social, the more effective the programmer. Highly productive programmers tend to display these anti-social traits to a high degree. Success in computing, therefore, tends to reinforce these qualities. In the worst cases, these traits may take on a pathological character to produce the hacker and other computing oddities.

The rapid gratification, fast progress, and high level of enjoyment found in computing may themselves deeply affect the personalities of programmers in other ways. These qualities may lead programmers to expect these in the rest of life. Given the personality traits that computing rewards and exaggerates, it is not surprising that users and managers may think that programmers should be locked up and kept out of sight, even if they do produce useful work.

3.4 Where do programmers come from?

Until recently, people became programmers only because they genuinely wanted to. It was difficult or expensive to gain access to computers. Courses were not widely available within the educational system; programmers largely educated themselves. Even today, programming is not something into which one can default. It takes conscious effort and hard work to become even moderately competent in programming. Because it is easy to ascertain if a program works, imposters are usually quickly unmasked by those with any real competence. Most programmers take great pride in their skills and work. 'Technical machismo' is an important aspect of their lives.

There is no standard way of becoming a professional programmer. Some education is generally required and a computer science degree may be useful, but is not essential. There is little professional impediment, however, to anyone who can program, even if they are not particularly competent (Boehm, 1988). Awkward questions about where and how they learned to program are not likely to be asked. Programmers and analysts with experience have a wide choice of potential employers. They can probably pick an area and then find a job, no matter what area. If they are willing to move to an urban area, e.g. New York or London, they probably can find a job paying 20 per cent more than their previous one within several days. Part of the arrogance of computer technologists is justified; they are unlikely to find themselves out of work for long.

3.5 Software managers

Software managers seem to have a hard time, although Couger and Zawaki (1980) found that they derived greater satisfaction from their jobs than other managers. Few software managers can be unaware of the risks and uncertainty of software development. Worse still, no matter what degree of success computer managers achieve in managing their operations, they never seem to be totally accepted by their management peers (Jones, 1986; King, 1983). While they tend to be excluded from the general organizational decision-making process, they are, paradoxically, increasingly expected to have a greater awareness of the strategic role of computing in their organization. At the same time, they are under pressure to achieve greater effectiveness in their day-to-day role.

Programmers who become managers usually do so with some sense of loss. As they become technically out of date (Weinberg, 1971), removed from the rapid gratification of programming, and lose their technical machismo, they tend to become insecure. Insecurity is amplified because programmers who become managers may not be trained for the role or dispositionally inclined to it (Boehm, 1987; Couger and Zawacki, 1980). Many of the personal qualities that made them successful as programmers may be unacceptable as managers. It is not surprising that few programmers who become managers ever reach board level in conventional companies.

Another common source of software managers is computer operations staff (Couger and Zawacki, 1980). Computer operations staff are not usually as technically competent as programmers. Their work is considerably less demanding intellectually and operations staff often lack the technical education of programmers. On the other hand, their work tasks are more akin to those of traditional management. Computer operations staff may be more inclined than programmers to assume management positions and functions (Couger and Zawacki, 1980). Consequently, they may prove more acceptable to company management as managers than programmers. From the programmers' point of view, however, operations may offer little technical insight into the problems of software development and managers coming from an operations background may have little credibility with programmers.

In some companies, non-technical staff may become software managers (Weinberg, 1971). The lot of the non-technical software manager can be especially miserable. Although the management of computing is in many respects similar to any other kind of management, programmers are notoriously difficult to handle (Weinberg, 1971). They are almost impossible to coerce and are adept at hoodwinking their management. Programmers resent being told how to do their jobs by those with less technical knowledge than they have. Lacking technical knowledge, in a technical field in which failure is so easily exposed, makes the position of the non-technical computing manager tenuous and exceedingly difficult. There is little chance of high management reward, either; only the hope for any early and fairly honourable escape from the 'software Siberia'.

3.6   Users

Users are the people who are expected to employ a particular computer system in their work. Computer professionals, of course, are extensive computer users. For this book, however, I would prefer to exclude this class of user from the discussion. Yourdon (1989) categorizes users as:

- Operational.
- Supervisory.
- Executive.

Prototyping is effective for dealing with all three of these user classes. Customer is a term sometimes employed as a synonym for user. I consider a customer, however, to be a person directly involved with purchasing the system. This person may or may not be a user of the system.

Most unfortunately, fear of the computer tends to be a major motivator of computer users. This manifests itself especially in worries about job security or of status displacement during the introduction of new computer systems (King, 1983). This fear may later be transformed into general negative attitudes towards computers and can manifest itself in uncertainty, poor performance, overt hostility, and even sabotage (Gibson and Nolan, 1974). User fear is a reaction that prototypers must become adept at recognizing and overcoming.

Other threats felt by users during the introduction of computer systems are (Bessant and Dickson, 1982; Galitz, 1980):

- Change of work content.
- Fear of impersonal surveillance.
- Loss of personal power and control.
- Feelings of inadequacy.

- Fear of failure.
- Fear of the unknown.
- Loss of habit and known environment.
- Disturbance of personal relationships.
- Lack of participation.

It is only reasonable to expect that some of the users' anxiety and hostility about computing will be transferred to software developers themselves. Even the most politically adept software developers must themselves contribute substantially to the worries and irritation of users, especially those concerned for their employment. Users are bound to be irritated by the following aspects:

- The relatively glamorous image of computing.
- Rumours or knowledge about the high pay of computing staff.
- The excellent employment prospects for computing staff.
- The seeming lack of loyalty that programmers have to the business (Couger and Zawacki, 1980).
- The intelligence, independence, ambition, and enthusiasm of computing staff.
- The odd personality traits and obviously separate culture of computing staff.

These irritants are bound to widen the division between user and developer. There truly is a culture gap and it is a wide one. Successful prototypers are the people who can act as the bridge between these two worlds. Prototypers have one big advantage over other approaches to development: they are on the side of the users.

3.7 Conclusion

The personal qualities that lead to success in programming may prove less satisfactory for coping with much of the rest of life, particularly dealing with users. Programmers may be strongly affected by the high degree of enjoyment, gratification, and progress that can be achieved from programming computers. Good pay and excellent employment prospects tend to make them almost immune to fears about unemployment. As a result, users and managers often find programmers difficult to deal with. 'Spoiled brats' is how one annoyed manager once described programmers to me. Technically competent and personally effective programmers are essential to successful prototyping. This is not necessarily an easy combination of skills to find in programmers.

Software managers have a difficult time. Not only is the job technically difficult, but they must liaise between the equally awkward users and programmers. To make matters worse, they are seldom treated with trust or respect by their peers or management. Some of this distrust and lack of respect may be deserved (King, 1983, p. 327). As a rule, software managers are unqualified for the positions they hold, either technically or dispositionally, and are under unrealistic pressure to perform well. Poor management is a major contributor to the failure of software developments. High-quality management, particularly in managing programmers and users, is vital to the success of prototyping.

Users are often the unwilling captives of management and software development. Management may use software developers as their 'shock troops' to effect change. Moreover, users are often not always particularly pleasant; their fear, petulance, and ignorance often reaches hysterical proportions. Sending the usual run of programmers or software managers to calm panicking or outraged users is somewhat like sending in more lions to help the Christians. Prototyping demands being able to defuse the fears of users and to develop enthusiasm and tolerance in an area where it is so seldom found.

Keeping users apart from software developers often seems one of the simplest and most effective means of keeping everyone happy. This is hardly a novel idea; 'highly skilled and creative. . . computer system programmers. . . are oriented to the technology. . . satisfaction and best performance may by assured by isolating them organisationally' (Gibson and Nolan, 1974, p. 82). While this may result in peace and quiet for management, it is not likely to result in any great progress for software development. The culture and communication gap is a wide one; something is needed desperately to help close it. Prototyping is the best answer I have seen yet.

One of the major strengths of prototyping is that it is an activity that often coincides with the natural inclinations of many of the people who are involved in software development. The major weakness of prototyping is that it depends almost totally on the calibre and personality of the people engaged in it. Good-quality people can make prototyping succeed, no matter what software tools are employed; low-quality people will make it fail. Therefore, a deep understanding of the human aspects of computing, even the vaguest aspects, is an essential element of the successful adoption, practice, and management of prototyping.

4

Custom software

This book is addressed mainly to organizations that produce custom software for their own use. Custom software is software produced specifically to meet the exact requirements of an organization. The software typically consists of simple operations carried out on complex databases (Talbot and Witty, 1983). There is likely to be a highly specialized — and often overly complex — interface between the software and its users. There may be a greater emphasis on 'style than substance' (Mason and Carey, 1983). No part of the custom software produced is necessarily unique, in its own right. It is generally the combination of database, function, user interface, and operating environment that produces the uniqueness of the custom software.

Although custom software may be produced by specialist external organizations, most organizations have an internal capability for producing custom software. Sometimes this capability may just be a member of staff who knows how to create spreadsheets. Often, though, this capability may be surprisingly large in terms of number of people and budget. It is not unusual to find organizations spending 10 per cent of their gross income in the generation, operation, and maintenance of software for internal purposes. Inventories of 5 000 000 source lines of program are not unusual in medium-sized companies. Large companies can have inventories 10 times that size (Jones, 1986). A significant proportion of this inventory may be custom software. If the standard dictum of '$10 per line' is applied, this inventory may be seen to represent a major investment.

4.1 Why produce custom software?

Custom software can be a way for organizations to gain significant competitive advantage. In many organizations, however, it also can be a major waste of effort, investment, and opportunity (Boehm, 1987). It is generally accepted that much software failure, custom or not, is related to the problems of designing software that meets the needs and requirements of users (Hollinde and Wagner, 1984; McCracken and Jackson, 1982). Consequently, any software development approach that addresses these problems must be of interest to custom software developers. Prototyping is a particularly appropriate approach for developing custom software internally.

The problem with custom software is that it appears to be the major area of software failure (Boehm, 1987). Examine almost any organization in which custom software is used and you are likely to find a long history of unhappy users, unsatisfied business needs, unanticipated costs, unmet schedules, and poor quality. You are also likely to find that computing staff are spending so much time maintaining existing custom applications that they are unable to meet demands for new ones. Any change of the software is likely to incur a substantial risk of causing more problems than benefits. It is not unusual in custom computing installations to find dozens of man-years of work being abandoned without hesitation or attempt at salvage.

Given the risks and problems of custom software, why do organizations continue to produce their own applications? Surely they would be better to buy pre-written software 'off the shelf' or to go without? The main reasons for producing custom software appear to be the following:

- Suitable pre-written software is not available for a specific business application. Organizations often see software as giving them some unique competitive function (Porter and Millar, 1985). Custom software is normally the only way in which this can be provided. This generally is a legitimate reason for writing custom software.
- Custom software can give users exactly what they want and need. In large organizations, it may be more economical to write software that exactly replaces existing functions than it is to change the manner in which the organization operates. This may be a legitimate reason for writing custom software in big companies. In smaller companies, rigorous and impartial cost analysis should be applied to decide if changing is more economical than writing special software.
- Coexistance with earlier custom software must be maintained. There is a strong tendency today to integrate software. Custom software may be so specialized that it becomes impossible to integrate it without writing more custom software. Interfacing requirements, however, can be standardized or at least simplified through good software design. Organizations should carefully examine their genuine requirements for software integration, however, before embarking on a custom development.
- Software may not exist for the computer hardware that the organization uses. Before selecting computer hardware, it is important to ensure that the necessary software is available and will continue to be available. It

may be more economical not to buy a certain type of computer than to buy one that has inadequate software. It may be cheaper to replace existing hardware that has inadequate software than it is to write custom software.

- Software has always been produced this way in the organization. Management in many organizations appears to be unaware that there is any other way to obtain their software. Often, the decision whether to buy or to write is left to the computing operation; the decision usually is to write the software rather than to buy it. Organizations should be more sceptical and knowledgeable about decisions to write software, rather than buy it.
- Internal software appears to be less expensive. Buying software usually exposes the costs of computing in a manner that is difficult to ignore, needs a positive decision, and may require vigorous justification. Internal software development, on the other hand, permits costs to be concealed in salaries and apparently modest operating expenditure and does not require a clear-cut decision. Organizations need to know the real cost of computing. An organization that does not want to know how much its computing costs probably deserves what it gets.

4.2   Externally produced software

Externally produced software comes in two forms: pre-written packages and custom development. The advantages and caveats of pre-written software packages are as follows:

- If properly evaluated, the buyer knows what he or she is getting in terms of function and performance. Evaluation, however, can consume a great deal of time (Jones, 1986).
- The software is ready immediately. That means organizations can plan reliably for installation and financing. Buyers must ensure, through evaluation, that the product really is ready. 'Vapourware' is a consistent feature of the package software market.
- The costs are known. Highly skilled staff are not needed for an unknown period to produce and maintain it. Buyers often underestimate other costs of acquisition, such as evaluation, training, maintenance, and 'optional extras'.
- If there are problems with the software, it is the vendor's responsibility and expense to fix it. The buyer is at the mercy of the supplier even for rectification. Enhancement is likely to be a slow process. The consequences of a supplier discontinuing a product or going out of business can be unfortunate.

The need for customization of packages is a serious problem. Most of the advantages of acquiring package software will be negated if customization is required (Jones, 1986).

The use of external developers to produce custom software theoretically has benefits similar to those of acquiring software packages:

- Fixed price contracts can be negotiated.
- Fixed delivery dates normally are expected.
- Maintenance is the developer's responsibility.

In my experience, there tends to be less friction when external developers, rather than internal staff, produce custom software. This may be because there is less contact between the users and the development staff. Everyone involved also tends to behave with greater reserve and politeness. Maintenance, after the usual initial flurry of bugs, tends to be less of a problem with external developers because perpetual enhancement is not expected by the users. User tolerance of problems seems to be higher with externally produced software and there is more obvious effort to 'work around' problems.

The results of externally produced custom software, however, appear to be more variable than those of internally produced custom software. It is not unusual for the results of externally produced custom software to be totally unacceptable. I suspect that users tend to get less satisfactory function and quality from externally produced software than from internally produced software. This is because external developers generally work from fixed, written specifications only. Unlike internally produced software, feedback is eliminated almost totally in external custom development after analysis.

External software has several implications for prototyping:

- User requirements for function alone can be satisfied more easily than is generally anticipated.
- Friction and uncertainty are very serious software development problems.
- If maintenance is readily available, users will make the most of it.
- Eliminating feedback in software development increases the risk of total failure.

4.3   Why does custom software fail?

Failures in custom software (Boehm, 1987) are rarely straightforward technical failures. Rather, they are the failure of the software to meet the needs and expectations of its users or of the business commissioning it. The successful custom software developer must strike a reasonable harmony among many conflicting factors. There is often a conflict between software that meets the needs of the business and software that meets the needs of the users. There also may be a conflict between the expectations and the genuine needs of both users and businesses.

Some of the factors that may contribute to the perception of failure by custom software developments, beyond the normal reasons for failure in software developments, are the following:

- Conflict between the business and users. The custom software developer is often the witting or unwitting agent of imposing new business needs and expectations upon the users. Here, the problems of change, even for the good, and bad business decisions tend to be blamed on the software developers by both company management and disgruntled users. As I have discussed, computer technologists are often the worst possible choice of change agents, from a personality point of view.
- Unreasonable expectations. The most legitimate reason for producing custom software is that it is not available in a suitable form anywhere else. High expectations about custom software are natural and the nature of the problems to be solved are likely to be inherently challenging. Unfortunately, there is a tendency for computing operations to oversell custom software projects and to create expectations that can never be met. Computer professionals have a disinclination to keep in contact with users, and traditional development methods discourage contact after analysis. This means there is little opportunity to scale expectations down as the software takes form. Where organizations treat plans as reality ('cast in iron' planning), it may be politically inexpedient to reduce expectations.
- Sub-competent computing staff and computer illiterate managers and users. Internal computing operations tend to encourage 'home-grown' software developers. These developers tend to be enthusiastic, almost totally untrained, and seriously lacking general knowledge about computer technology. These enthusiasts tend to use the tools they have and know and often produce amazing results. The results, however, may be idiosyncratic, unmaintainable, non-standard, unreliable, or incapable of being interfaced. The home-grown developers tend to remain in their organizations, possibly because their skills are inadequate outside. Eventually, they become embedded in the decision-making process for computing.

    The lack of computer literacy among managers is well documented (Coplin et al., 1986). Without proper management constraints and control, the home-grown experts usually play on their initial success. This lasts until a major catastrophe is precipitated or they recognize their limitations. Home-grown experts usually build their computer operations into a fortress which no outsiders, including users, may penetrate and so expose their weaknesses.
- Underestimation of difficulty, resources, costs, and time-scales (W. Myers, 1989). It is my view, based on experience and review of the literature, that it is impossible to estimate accurately the problems, times, and costs of software development until after the development is finished. In

any event, as part of the oversell of a development project, it is normal to scale cost and time-scale estimations to meet the expectations of the business and users.

It is unusual, in my experience, for software developers, especially internal ones, to reject interesting projects merely because they believe they cannot meet the time-scales and budget. Normally, they simply adjust their predictions to match expectations and hope that everything will turn out right in the end. Their managements abet this reaction because they expect their computer operations to respond favourably to their requests. They lack sufficient technical knowledge to understand whether their requests of the predictions of their computing staff are reasonable.

- Imposition of applications knowledge by computer staff on the users. This tendency is particularly prevalent in internal computing organizations, especially those run by home-grown computing experts. Because of their varied exposure to many aspects of the organization, computing staff generally come to know a lot about their host organization. They genuinely may have a better general understanding of the business than most users and some general management. This understanding can cause conflict between computing staff and users or lead to strong resentment on both sides. It also may result in delivery of more functions than the users want or can handle. It can cause misguided imposition of the software producers' views of the business on the business.

- Maintenance 'critical mass'. Most software requires, over its lifetime, from two to three times as much manpower to maintain and enhance as it does to create it (Boehm, 1981). The problem is well described by Nolan (1979), 'Base level systems cannot support higher level systems. . . . Maintenance of the existing, poorly designed systems begins to occupy 70% to 80% of the productive time of programmers and systems analysts.' Maintenance is an inherently difficult and expensive activity (King, 1983). Worse still, programmers, even experienced ones, are generally unable to understand large programs, even those written by themselves, and remove all the errors (Sengler, 1983).

As software gets older, the need for enhancement usually becomes much greater than the need to rectify software errors. The maintenance problem is exacerbated by the snowball effect of complexity. Even with good documentation and design, it soon becomes difficult to predict accurately the effects of any change to the software in a major system. As a consequence, a programming operation of fixed size and average competence can normally produce more software in four to five years than it can maintain. Some computing operations refuse to see that they have reached critical mass, even when it is obvious, and continue to produce software. Others refuse to admit it and employ all sorts of defensive delaying and hedging tactics to avoid new commitments and to underplay problems with existing software.

4.4 Discussion

A custom software operation is a bit like running a gourmet restaurant. Customers expect eveything to be exactly right. Imagine taking your friends out for an expensive meal. The food is delicious, but the waiter drops one of the main courses down the back of your best friend. The chef rushes out and shows you his cooking school credentials. He explains that the dinner was carefully planned, came from the best possible recipe, was cooked in the most modern ovens, and requires a minimum amount of washing up. The head waiter then hands you the bill. Do you think that you would come back to this restaurant again? If you knew that something like this was going to happen at least half the time, don't you think you might take your friends out to a 'fast food' restaurant instead?

Custom software developers, especially internal ones, are often working in situations in which many factors hinder their progress. In my experience, internal custom software operations are generally able to produce, technically, the software that their users and organizations demand and need. They are unable, however, to produce it as rapidly and smoothly as it is wanted. The process of internal software development often causes many problems: delays and cost overruns seem almost inevitable, and demands for enhancement of successful software are likely to be never-ending. The traditional software development approach has not been successful in reducing these problems.

No matter how successful the custom software operation has been, if maintenance critical mass is reached, then progress ceases. At this point, the internal developers and all their works fall into disrepute with their users and management. The operation is then stamped as a failure. Avoiding maintenance critical mass, therefore, must be a major consideration of preventing custom software failure. It is not enough to get the software right, it also must be able to be enhanced as long as it is needed. Prototyping is valuable in avoiding maintenance critical mass because it helps produce software of higher quality that may be more easily maintained (Boehm *et al.*, 1984) than that produced through other approaches.

The perception of failure of custom software is widespread (Boehm, 1987). Custom software often fails, even though it meets the actual function needs and requirements for which it was developed. The *raison d'être* of custom software is to meet the total needs, requirements, and expectations of the business and the users. Inability to do this in the custom software arena is likely to result in failure, no matter what its reasons. It is important that custom software developers recognize that creating the perception of success is as important as producing a technically excellent product. Prototyping is an approach that can supply both the reality and perception of success in custom software development.

5
Introduction to prototyping

A software prototype is a preliminary version or a model of all or part of a system before full commitment is made to develop it (IT-STARTS, 1989a). A software prototype can also be part or all of a system that is developed and delivered using an iterative approach in which users are involved. Prototyping is the process of creating a prototype.

The objective of creating prototypes is to assist, in some way, the development of target or delivered systems. Major issues of software development (Fig. 5.1) that can be addressed by prototyping are elicitation, demonstration, and evaluation of the following:

- Data requirements and structure.
- Function requirements.
- Operation and performance.
- Organizational needs and issues.

In normal usage, a prototype is a trial model or a preliminary version of a product (Sykes, 1976). In conventional engineering, prototyping at reduced scale, with simplified versions of products or with a pre-production product, is a long-established tradition. The idea of producing a building, a bridge, an automobile, or an aeroplane without a prototype or model is almost inconceivable (Jones, 1986). Prototyping at an early stage in the development of a product allows evaluation and adjustment before the design is finalized.

On the face of it, the analogy between prototyping in engineering and prototyping in software appears to be a valid one. The analogy may be facile, however, because the nature of the software is different from that of conventionally engineered products (Floyd, 1984), even one-off products such as bridges. The differences are as follows:

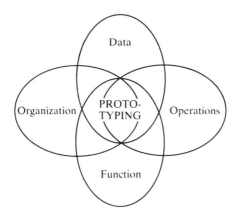

Figure 5.1 Major issues addressed by prototyping

- The mutability of the software prototype is much greater than that of an engineering prototype.
- Unlike many engineering products, software is not manufactured, but is a one-off product. Replication is not a problem as it is in engineering. The problem in software is producing the prototype.
- Software products often have characteristics that are unclear at the beginning of the prototype development.
- The relationship between the software product and its prototype often is unclear. The prototype may even become the product itself.

Iterative or incremental development (Graham, 1989) might often be a more accurate term than software prototyping. Nevertheless, the term 'prototyping' is so widely used, even if not totally accurate, that I will use it in this book.

5.1 Definitions

The definition of prototyping is a loose one. There are a number of other terms commonly associated with the subject, some of which are relevant and some of which are not. The following list gives, in alphabetical order, some of these terms:

- Breadboard. This is a prototype with a high degree of function, but a limited user interface. Breadboard prototypes are valuable for estimating performance or efficiency or for developing functions or data structures experimentally.
- Design. This is the stage in software development where the form of the system is planned. Prototyping is not a design technique. Good design is

essential for effective prototyping and prototyping may be an effective means of evaluating design.

- Evolutionary development. This is a prototype that becomes the delivered system without a substantial amount of rework. Evolutionary development can be employed to address all the issues of development (Fig. 5.1). This form of prototyping is discussed in greater detail below.
- Incremental development. This is a strategy in which the delivered system is developed in small steps. Each step is self-contained in its software and documentation (Graham, 1989). Delivery to the user may also be incremental. There is no implication that prototyping must be employed in incremental development and delivery. This strategy may, however, be a means of managing prototyping.
- Mock-up. This is a static, sub-functional prototype that demonstrates the appearance the system should take. Mock-ups may become 'fleshed out' and become a part of the delivered system. Mock-ups typically address the more cosmetic issues of software development, although they may be valuable for eliciting functional requirements (Fig. 5.1) from users and developing user interfaces.
- Model. This is a software abstraction of limited scope. It may be inanimate. Models are often general-purpose software tools that are applied to test specific cases. Models normally would not become part of the delivered system, although their internal mechanisms might be used. Models tend to be useful for testing function and determining data structure (Fig. 5.1).
- Simulation. This is a dynamic, mathematical, or algorithmical representation of an activity. Simulators, like models, are often general-purpose software tools applied to specific problems. Simulators normally would not become part of the delivered system. Simulation is valuable mainly for estimating performance (Fig. 5.1).
- Skeleton. This is a prototype of wide scope that is used to evaluate or elucidate general rules and constraints for the delivered system. Functions and data are more or less complete, but rudimentary. The skeleton may become the framework of the delivered system. Skeleton prototypes are useful for eliciting function and data requirements (Fig. 5.1).
- Testing and evaluation. These terms are similar, except that testing has a more limited connotation of determining the correctness of something. Evaluation implies determination of value, as well as correctness. For example, a computer solution may be technically correct, but it may have no value to the user because he or she cannot use it. Prototyping is not a testing technique; it can, however, greatly assist evaluation.
- Throw-away. This is a prototype that is redeveloped using a conventional software approach. This type of prototype is discussed in greater detail below. The throw-away approach is typically used to elicit function and data requirements (Fig. 5.1).

- User development. This is where users develop their own software. User-developers tend to use informal software development approaches, but this is not prototyping. User developers can be very efficient prototypers, however, because of their specialist knowledge.

5.2 The basic prototype

The types of target or production systems addressed in this book are custom software applications, delivered to end-users within conventional organizations. In this area of prototyping, users are almost always involved directly in evaluating the software.

I would prefer to restrict my use of the word 'prototyping' to the activities (Fig. 5.2) of needs elicitation, software implementation, and user evaluation of the implementation which result in the creation of the final prototype. The term 'delivery' is reserved for the activities associated with creating a target system from the implemented prototype. Typical delivery activities are documentation and training.

The traditional and software engineering approaches follow the prototyping schematic in a very general way. The main difference between prototyping and the other approaches is that iteration or feedback can happen at any point in prototyping. Feedback is not supposed to be needed after design in the traditional or software engineering software development approaches. In prototyping, there is also an implication that the prototype itself will serve as the formal statement of needs. The feature that may help distinguish from anarchical development approaches is that feedback comes from needs elicitation in concert with the users.

5.3 Prototyping strategies

There are two major prototyping strategies (Parbst, 1984); throw-away and evolutionary. Although other authors (e.g. Hekmatpour and Ince, 1986) make finer distinctions, I see no particular value to most software developers in these.

Throw-away or throw-it-away (Hekmatpour and Ince, 1986) prototypes (Fig. 5.3) are those in which the prototype is redeveloped or translated into another form before the target system is delivered (Smith, 1981). The translation process may be considered either a part of prototyping or a part of delivery. Typically, the software designer uses the throw-away prototype as a total or partial substitute for the analysis stage in the traditional development cycle (Lugi, 1988). Strictly speaking, no part of the throw-away prototype should be reused in any form.

Evolutionary prototypes (Fig. 5.4) are prototypes that themselves become delivered target systems. Ince (1987) differentiates between evolutionary and incremental prototypes, but the distinction appears to be largely academic.

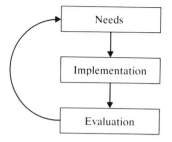

Figure 5.2 A simple prototype

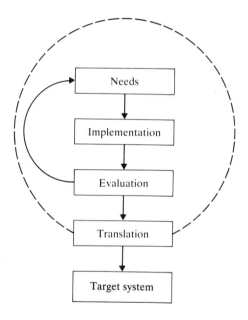

Figure 5.3 A schematic of throw-away prototyping

Evolutionary prototyping might be more appropriately called incremental development (Graham, 1989). Evolutionary prototyping is much further removed from the definition of engineering prototyping than throw-away prototyping (Floyd, 1984) and therefore much more contentious.

There has been considerable emphasis in the literature on the speed of prototyping (Jones, 1986) and on 'rapid prototyping' (e.g. Tanik and Yeh, 1989). In my view, this is a seriously misguided emphasis. If staff are expected to produce software rapidly, at the expense of all other qualities, then the quality and maintainability of their work is bound to suffer

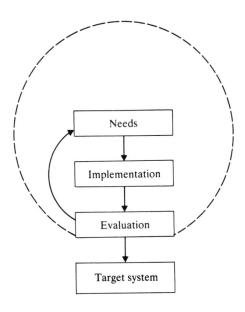

Figure 5.4 A schematic of evolutionary prototyping

(Boehm, 1988). Emphasis on prototyping should be less about the speed of development and more about involving the users throughout the development. Speed is valuable, but prototyping is prototyping, whether the time-scale is one of hours or one of years.

5.4 Scope of prototyping

Prototypes, either throw-away or evolutionary, can be used for entire systems or for sub-sets of them (partial prototypes). Prototypes can be internal or external from the viewpoint of the users, although traditionally they tend to focus upon the external surfaces of systems. Prototypes also may exhibit either 'horizontal' or 'vertical' functionality (Fig. 5.5).

Horizontal prototypes cannot perform a full application. In other words, users cannot use them to perform a complete task. Typical horizontal prototypes are breadboard and mock-up prototypes. Horizontal prototypes, especially partial ones, have long been employed by software developers, and they generally prove beneficial. Their effect on software development is not profound, however, because they do not permit users to evaluate their software needs fully.

Vertical prototypes, both partial and complete, are of much greater interest than horizontal prototypes. Vertical prototypes exhibit complete functionality, although their application extent may be limited. They also

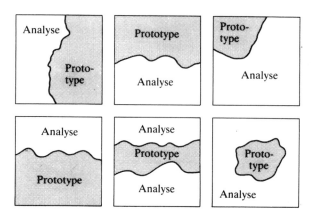

Figure 5.5   Scope of prototyping

may be deficient in performance or final appearance. Nevertheless, a user should be able to carry out, realistically, a complete work task. Vertical prototypes, therefore, will normally have the following:

- A user interface.
- Algorithms or data manipulations.
- Data structures and storage.

Vertical prototypes are interesting because they permit users to evaluate their needs realistically. The effect on software development of being able to evaluate user needs in this way is both profound and beneficial. Vertical prototypes are also more suitable for inclusion in delivered systems (Graham, 1989).

5.5   The reality of prototyping

What is the reality of prototyping? The case studies (pages 165–190) attempt to impart a realistic flavour of what prototyping is really like. A typical scenario, briefly, is that the management of an organization decides that they wish an application to be done by computer. The software manager is instructed to this effect and asked to establish the feasibility and cost of developing the application. After doing this, and assuming that a favourable conclusion is reached, the software manager is told to proceed with development.

The software manager first must decide if the application is an appropriate one for prototyping. The next decision to be made, using the software manager's judgement and experience, is whether a throw-away or an evolutionary prototype is more appropriate. The decision is also made as to whether the prototype should be partial or complete. The software manager instructs the prototype developer (the prototyper) or developers about their roles and objectives in the project. The wise software manager will prepare a written brief outlining the objectives of the development.

The software manager (prototype manager) must also arrange the 'raw materials' of the prototype: prototype developer (prototyper), hardware, software, and users. These arrangements are not always made in a formal way, especially in small organizations. Arranging users, however, almost always requires the cooperation of the user management. Once all the materials are arranged, the prototyper and the users discuss the application. The prototyping and other managers may also be involved in these discussions, which tend to be informal, but intense.

The prototyper then goes away and produces some software. The amount of software produced is usually left to the discretion of the prototyper. This software, often screens on a video display, is shown to the user. The user comments on what is presented and on what is missing. The prototyper then goes back and develops some more software. The implementation process (Fig. 5.6) normally iterates until the user is satisfied or management stops prototype development.

Frequently, software is produced that permits the user to do real or realistic work. The user or users may begin to use the software in their work, even before the prototype is finished. If this happens, the prototype may become the target system. If this is planned, then this is evolutionary prototyping. If it is not planned, then this is bad management; problems are likely to ensue. If a throw-away strategy is adopted, then the prototype will be employed as a specification for a target system. Redevelopment can proceed as normal.

5.6 Discussion

Prototyping is the process of producing a trial version of software before developing a final system. The prototype is evaluated, often by users, and improved until it meets the needs for which it was intended. Once developed, the prototype may be translated before delivery. In this case the prototype serves as a specification for the target system. This style of prototyping is called throw-away prototyping. Throw-away prototyping is a well-accepted practice in software development (IT-STARTS, 1989a), although not necessarily widely practised. This style of prototyping is valuable to organizations, especially where custom software is being developed for end-users.

Evolutionary prototyping is a radical approach to software development. In this approach, the prototype is employed as the target system itself, without translation. There is a strong implication that the prototype will evolve during its life. This style of prototyping is not widely accepted (IT-STARTS, 1989a), although it may be more widely practised than is generally imag-

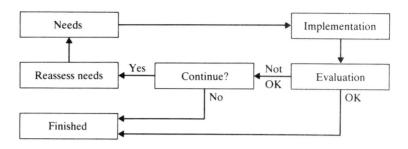

Figure 5.6   The prototyping process

ined. As Mathiassen (1984) says, 'There is no difference between what we have here called prototyping, and what we have been practising all the time.'

Evolutionary prototyping can be an acceptable approach to software development in many cases. It must be carefully evaluated by organizations before attempting to adopt it. If adopted, careful practice and management are required. There also is a definite requirement for careful software tool selection if evolutionary prototyping is considered for adoption because of the implication that the final software must operate efficiently and harmoniously in the target environment.

There should be no misconceptions about prototyping. It is not an undisciplined, amateur do-it-yourself approach (Mason and Carey, 1983). The skill and discipline of the prototyper is the key to effective prototype development. Prototyping is not a suitable approach for computing amateurs or beginners; it requires staff with the best available technical and interpersonal skills. For multi-developer prototyping projects, a high degree of management skill is also required. If any of these skills are not available, then prototyping becomes highly risky.

Part Two
Rationale for prototyping

In this section, 'Rationale for prototyping', I attempt to show dialectically that the prototyping approach is not illogically founded. I also try to show that the potential benefits of prototyping can be substantial. The problems associated with prototyping are also discussed in considerable detail. I do consider, however, that most of these problems are related to software in general, rather than to prototyping specifically.

The approaches and problems of the traditional, analytically based software development are presented in the middle of this section. The role of prototyping in the traditional approach is considered. My conclusion is that the major impediment to adopting prototyping in organizations that employ the traditional software development approach is likely to be their own computing staff. The reaction of their computer staff against prototyping may be largely based on emotion, rather than technical issues. This is not to imply that this emotional impediment is irrelevant or trivial, but rather to indicate that overcoming it will require an appropriate approach.

The latter part of this section may be perceived by some as a prejudiced and violent attack on software engineering. I have attempted to put my points forward with strength in an attempt to achieve some balance. I am neither prejudiced against software engineering nor are my reservations about software engineering unsupported by other authors. I have been particularly influenced by the low-key, but distressingly negative conclusions of Webster's (1988) comprehensive study of methodologies. I have long had serious worries that the emphasis of software engineering seems to be heading towards simplistic, mechanical solutions for what I perceive as a complex set of human problems.

6
Prototyping benefits and problems

There is evidence, unfortunately of the variety typical to computing, that prototyping can improve the efficiency and quality of software development (Boehm *et al.*, 1984). Prototyping seems particularly effective for the elicitation, definition, and communication of application needs and user requirements (Boar, 1984; Mason and Carey, 1983). There may be problems associated with prototyping, however. Organizations evaluating the adoption of prototyping are advised to weigh the pros and cons in their particular context before making any decisions.

6.1 Benefits of prototyping

Experimental evidence (Boehm, 1984, 1988; Jordan *et al.*, 1989), such as it is, suggests that prototyping, when compared to traditional approaches, may halve the development effort required. Dearnley and Mayhew (1984) suggest that cost reductions of an order of magnitude can be achieved by using prototyping instead of the traditional development approach. The evidence also suggests that substantially smaller programs may result (Boehm *et al.*, 1984). The case study of Jones (1986), however, indicates that the quantative benefits of prototyping, while substantial, are more modest.

Other preceived benefits of prototyping are the following:

- Users may be unable to articulate or understand their applications in a computing context (Mason and Carey, 1983). Correspondingly, software developers may find it easier and more effective to communicate with users through prototypes than through other means. Prototypes are a simple, comprehensive, complete, and unambiguous means of communication between users and developers.

53

- Prototyping gives a better appreciation of the problems and benefits of the software before installation. There always is something concrete that can be seen and evaluated by management.
- Prototyping provides rapid reinforcement and gives greater stimulus throughout development. Users can see their ideas being fed back rapidly into the development process. This engenders feelings of user ownership about the software being developed.
- Prototyping makes it possible to 'down scale' expectations to realistic proportions after the inevitable high expectations and over-selling at the beginning of the project.
- Often, parts of the prototype can be employed to gain business advantage before full delivery or serve to provide a stop-gap function (Salter, 1989).
- Staff training and education can proceed before final system delivery.
- Prototyping makes software development easier where organizations are multi-lingual. When users and developers speak different human languages or speak them indifferently, this poses an additional barrier to effective software development. Prototyping provides an unambiguous and efficient means of communication, even where different languages are spoken.
- There is a wide culture and communications gap between users and computing technologists (Hekmatpour and Ince, 1986; McCracken and Jackson, 1982). Prototyping is a practical and inexpensive means of bridging this gap.
- Prototyping involves users and software developers directly in the enjoyable (King, 1983) and creative aspects of computing.
- In prototyping, testing and rectification of design and implementation begins early (Mason and Carey, 1983) and proceeds throughout the development. Errors may cost as much as several orders of magnitude more to rectify in the later stages of development than they do in earlier stages (Boehm, 1983; Boehm et al., 1984).
- Prototyping allows users and developers to change their minds, without stigma or loss of face, at any point during the development. Analytical and software engineering approaches discourage the changing of requirements after an early stage in development (Bates, 1989; Mason and Carey, 1983).
- Prototyping may produce smaller and higher-quality software with better user interfaces and less 'gold plating' (Boehm and Papaccio, 1988; Boehm et al., 1984; Hekmatpour and Ince, 1986; Ince, 1988; Jones, 1986).
- There is some evidence (Boehm et al., 1984; Jones, 1986; Luqi and Berzins, 1988) that prototyping results in software that is easier to maintain than that produced through conventional development approaches.
- Where evolutionary prototyping is adopted, there may be a reduced need for a separate maintenance stage. This may make maintenance simpler

because it reduces the emotional and organizational obstacles of contracting separately for maintenance and of maintenance moving outside the immediate environment in which the software was developed.

- Prototyping flattens peak manpower requirements and reduces the 'deadline rush' (Boehm *et al.*, 1984) for resources.
- Bates (1989) suggests that prototyping is the most natural development method for students. The implication may be that prototyping is the natural style of most programmers.
- Prototyping overcomes developers' inability to understand complex systems, except as small components. It permits a natural trial-and-error approach to developing complex systems. Prototypes permit developers to learn about applications and to experiment with them (Bates, 1989).

6.2 Prototyping problems

Some of the perceived problems of prototyping (Boehm *et al.*, 1984; Hekmatpour and Ince, 1986; Luqi and Berzins, 1988) are the following:

- Configuration and version control of prototypes may be more difficult than with conventional development. Prototyping can result in many trial systems. It is possible to get versions mixed or to be unable to recover a prototype to an earlier version. Software tools are available to help configuration and version control. There is no substitute for good documentation and strong management. Prototyping places no impediment in the way of either.
- Keeping documentation current may be difficult in prototyping because of its rapidly changing and iterative nature. It is difficult to maintain documentation in a reasonable condition during prototyping. Good management and a professional attitude for prototypers is essential to ensuring that documentation is kept in a reasonable condition.
- Maintaining discipline and objectives in the development team is difficult (Ince, 1989) because of the fluid nature and constant demands of prototyping. If the prototype development is not reasonably managed, it is possible for developers to become distracted from the legitimate goals of the prototype. I would observe that it is much more difficult to maintain discipline and objectives in good staff in a static and unchallenging situation than it is to control them when they are fully and deeply committed to a dynamic project.
- Planning and allocating resources is difficult in an environment dealing with uncertainty and the unknown (Livesey, 1984; Mayhew *et al.*, 1989). Uncertainty and the unknown are what makes it difficult to plan, not prototyping. Almost all software developments exist in a 'sea of uncertainty'. As soon as this is recognized, planning becomes difficult. Planning is a useful way of thinking about the future: it should not however, be confused with the actual future itself.

- Integration with and interface to other systems may be more difficult with prototypes (Boehm, 1988; Boehm *et al.*, 1984). If internal systems standards are not maintained during prototyping, it may prove difficult or even impossible to interface the prototype with existing or future systems. The same may be said of conventional development. Good management is needed in both to ensure that standards are maintained (Bedgen, 1984).
- It is possible for designs to be less coherent with prototyping than with traditional methods. Prototyping permits dealing with complex and ill-defined problems in an unstructured manner. As a result, it may be more difficult to impose a careful design on the prototype. Again, organizations must make decisions: do they want elegantly designed software or do they want software that meets the needs of its users?
- Testing may be neglected in prototypes. There is a danger in prototyping that testing will be left exclusively to the users. This is unacceptable proto-typing practice because users may not find all the bugs. Prototyping is not about users debugging programs, but rather about presenting users with working software so that they can evaluate it within the context of their own understanding and logic of the functions being computerized.
- Prototypes may be less robust then traditional systems. This worry is based on the misconception that prototyping means 'dirty' program-ming. The essence of prototyping is iterative development with the users, not software anarchy. There is no implication that quality and testing in prototyping should suffer. If it does, this is the result of bad management, not of using the prototyping approach.
- Inefficient operation of prototypes is a concern (Mason and Carey, 1983). Prototypes are more concerned with form than with function. Prototypes, therefore, may be less efficient than systems designed with efficiency in mind from the beginning. Unsuitable prototyping tools are also a source of potential inefficiency. Careful tool selection can alleviate some problems with efficiency. Inevitably, trade-offs are necessary. An organization must decide for itself whether efficiency is more important than meeting the needs of users.
- Prototypes may be unsuitable for translation into larger systems. The designs produced by prototyping may be too narrowly focused or the tools employed unsuitable for scaling the prototype up into a full-sized, working system. Suitable prototyping tools are an effective means of reducing this problem (Boar, 1984). Experience, knowledge of the principles of design, good testing techniques, and suitable software tools are the best antidotes to this problem.
- There are many more opportunities for strained relationships between users and computing technologists. Prototyping emphasizes and depends on much more contact with users and developers than traditional methods. If the users and developers are unsuited or ill-prepared for this contact,

severe problems may develop and prototyping may prove a failure. One of the key issues of prototyping is the selection of suitable staff. Keeping relationships working smoothly is a legitimate management function.

- Prototyping will disrupt or distract users. The much greater involvement of users in software development is bound to take considerable time and effort on their part. On the other hand, software that does not meet their needs is likely to have a more disruptive effect. It is important, however, that the necessary disruption is planned for in the users' work load and that time spent involved in prototyping is not merely squeezed in.
- Prototyping may result in less planning for delivery and maintenance. Because of the emphasis on meeting immediate user and business needs, developers may defer planning until it is too late. Good management is needed to ensure that planning is carried out at the proper time in both prototyping and traditional development.
- Prototyping cannot be used where external software developers are involved. If external developers work to fixed-price contracts, then they are likely to demand fixed specifications. Introducing prototyping into this environment may prove difficult (Graham, 1989; Mayhew et al., 1989).

All these reservations about prototyping are valid to some degree or another. All these problems can be reduced to reasonable proportions, however, by good management and intelligent selection of staff, tools, and projects. It must be pointed out, too, that the objections about prototyping are equally true of all software development approaches, including the traditional or software engineering ones. Poor staff, tools, and management will, inevitably, lead to poor results.

6.3 Where to adopt prototyping

Prototyping is a particularly appropriate software development approach in the following circumstances (Budgen, 1984):

- The functions of an application are not completely understood.
- The mechanisms for providing a function or their exact behaviour within an application are not completely understood.
- The user interface is not well defined or an application is highly interactive with its users.
- More than one solution is proposed and the alternatives require realistic assessment.
- It is desired that users should become involved in the development of the application.
- Users lack sufficient skill, time, or inclination to become involved in traditional analysis.

- The time to develop the software is likely to be longer than the specifications remain valid (Hollinde and Wagner, 1984).
- Hardware and software architectures are not firm (Graham, 1989).
- It is expedient to be seen to be producing working software before delivery.

Prototyping, of some form or another, could probably be employed in any application. This may be true from a technical point of view, but I would not recommend prototyping as a primary development approach in the following situations:

- Where iteration or experimentation is not possible. There are some applications that happen only once or are such that an experimental approach is impractical (i.e. life threatening). Here, the computer system must work the first time it is run.
- Where litigation could arise from software development errors (Boehm *et al.*, 1984). Prototyping on a large scale is not generally accepted within conservative sectors of the computing industry. Its use might not be defensible in court. The border between hacking and prototyping is not yet clearly established. Were a prototyper to end up in court, the plaintiff would probably have no trouble finding experts to testify against him or her.
- Where the organizational culture is totally immersed in the analytical styles of software development. Here, the opposition is likely to be so strong that prototyping will be made to fail, no matter what, or the effort involved will not be worth the results.
- Where security is a major design issue (Mathiassen, 1984). A typical example might be financial accounting systems where a high degree of compartmentalization is required.

I would not attempt to do more than introduce prototyping in a limited manner in other situations, such as the following:

- When the requirements are genuinely well known and well documented (Boehm *et al.*, 1984). For example, in a simple redevelopment of existing software. Here, prototyping probably would be a waste of time. It also might result in spurious changes being made to the software.
- When the application is exceedingly complex. Prototyping is not sufficiently well understood to be defended as a primary development technique in very large, highly complex software developments.
- Where the quality of development staff is low or where their personalities are obviously unsuited to direct interaction with users. Such staff are likely to cause many more problems than they solve during prototyping.
- Where the client's hardware and software can be seen to be unsuited to the task. This should only have a limiting effect, however, rather than a totally inhibiting effect on prototyping. For example, I have prototyped

successfully using systems based on paper tape assemblers and on FORTRAN punched cards.

6.4 What prototyping does not address

In speaking to computer professionals, I frequently detect some expectation that prototyping will lower development costs. This aspect is not extensively discussed in the literature. Jones (1986, p. 196) suggests that prototyping might lower overall costs by about 15 per cent. One might expect that the smaller programs produced would result in lower programming costs. This is naïve since prototyping staff must be more skilled, and hence are probably more expensive. The nature of prototyping is such that I would expect any budget allocated to be used up producing software of higher quality and greater functionality. In any event, there is insufficient evidence about proto-typing and costs to make any conclusions.

Prototyping is strongly connected to the design process but it is not part of it. Prototyping is a valuable approach for providing input, especially from non-technical people, into the design process. It also is a useful means of testing and evaluating the output from the design process. No matter how useful it may prove to the design process, prototyping is not a design tech-nique or methodology. For example, prototyping is extremely valuable for testing database structures under realistic conditions, but it cannot be expected to reveal the database structures.

6.5 Discussion

The benefits of prototyping are fairly well documented in the literature (e.g. Hekmatpour and Ince, 1986). There is evidence that substantial gains in software quality and productivity can be realized by using prototyping (e.g. Boehm et al., 1984). Prototyping appears particularly appropriate where cus-tom software is developed for end-users. There are other applications, too, in which prototyping may be extremely valuable.

The problems of prototyping appear to be fairly well understood. None of the problems appear particularly serious or unique to prototyping. There are some application areas where prototyping can be seen to be inappropriate, but these are clearly indicated. The most serious problems appear to be related to the high quality of staff required for prototyping and the possible adverse emotional reaction of computing staff to prototyping.

The adoption of throw-away prototyping within an organization should not be a difficult decision to make. This style of prototyping is generally accepted as being a legitimate part of conservative software development 'best practice' (IT-STARTS, 1989b). Evolutionary prototyping, however, is a radical departure from traditional software development practice. Advo-cates of evolutionary prototyping claim that this approach simply addresses the reality of many software developments. Detractors of evolutionary prototyping claim, with some justification, that it is an attempt to legitimize 'hacking'.

Evolutionary prototyping is not, at present, considered part of best programming practice. This does not necessarily mean that this will always be the case or even that organizations should not use evolutionary prototyping now. What seems certain is that all forms of prototyping require talented staff and that careful management is necessary to prevent degeneration of prototyping development into disorder. Organizations lacking talented staff and capable management are probably better off sticking to traditional methods than embarking on any type of prototyping. In fact, organizations seriously lacking those qualities might be well advised not to engage in any software development at all.

7
Prototyping and traditional software development

Software traditionally has been produced using the 'waterfall' (Boehm, 1987; Graham, 1989), analytical, or specified (Boehm *et al.*, 1984) approach to software development. In my interpretation of the traditional approach (Fig. 7.1) the full software design is created during the early stages of development. Development is mainly in one direction only; iteration is not a part of the overall approach.

Feasibility (Fig. 7.1) is generally a cursory examination in all approaches to software development. The cursory treatment is unfortunate because too many developments proceed that might better be aborted at this stage. Usually, though, determination of feasibility is left to software development staff. They, quite naturally, focus upon the technical feasibility of the application. Software development staff rarely give serious consideration to business or human feasibility.

Analysis (Fig. 7.1) is the point at which user and business requirements are determined. In the most unimaginative interpretation of the traditional approach, this may be regarded as the only legitimate point for user input into system design. Occasionally, some prototyping of input screens or reports may be employed at this stage. Users and managers are expected to know and communicate all the functions and features the software should have, even though they may have little or no knowledge of computers. In reality, analysts tend to rely heavily on their own insights and experiences to produce definitions of requirements. Users and managers are then shown designs and plans on paper and are asked to approve the designs. Once these are approved, development proceeds.

Design (Fig. 7.1) takes needs and requirements elicited from the users by the analyst to produce the detailed plan for implementation. It is usual, as well, for designers to rely heavily on their own experience of similar appli-

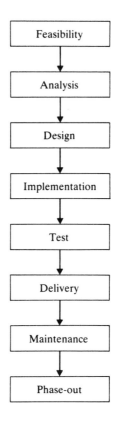

Figure 7.1   A schematic of the traditional software development approach

cations. The design may or may not be produced by the person who analysed the requirements. The blueprint produced by the design phase is intended for the implementors of the software. Users and non-technical management may be asked to comment upon the design or even give formal approval. Once approved, it is expected that the design will not need to be changed.

Implementation and testing (Fig. 7.1) come long after analysis and design. These stages should be isolated from the users in the traditional software development approach. Programmers work only from the design blueprint. In practice, a great deal of latitude may be permitted or accepted. Programmers may inject many of their own ideas during implementation. Testing at this stage means testing for functional correctness at a detailed level, not user evaluation.

Delivery (Fig. 7.1) is the point at which the user first comes in contact with the actual software. There is likely to be considerable responsibility placed on users to carry out acceptance testing in parallel with their training. Users are under pressure to accept the system as rapidly as possible. Where developers are part of a relatively small internal organization, immediate rejection of the software is not normally a real option. This is because of the adverse financial and political consequences of an outright rejection.

Maintenance (Fig. 7.1) in the traditional software development approach consists of two different, but usually simultaneous activities: rectification and enhancement. Rectification is correcting the errors of design and implementation in the delivered software. Enhancement is changing the implementation to meet new or newly discovered requirements after delivery. Enhancements may account for 40 per cent of the total maintenance effort (Nosek, 1984). It is significant that maintenance rarely goes through the traditional development cycle, i.e. there are no feasibility, requirements, or design stages. In effect, maintenance tends to degenerate into uncontrolled incremental development.

Phase-out (Fig. 7.1) or termination may not be formally considered in the software plan. The consequences of not considering termination at the start can have serious effects on the organization. Unsuccessful software is likely to be disposed of covertly. In this case, nothing is learned and the loss is unaccounted. Successful software continues to be 'improved' until it becomes unmaintainable. Replacement is not considered a natural event in the life of software, but rather something unnatural and undesirable. Phase-out is an aspect that should also be considered in prototyping.

7.1 The fatal flaws

Prototyping is a term derived loosely from conventional engineering. The traditional, analytical software development approach has an even stronger engineering analogy: the blueprint (Iivari, 1984). In the blueprinting process, designers create the blueprint or detailed plan for implementation from their analysis of the needs and requirements of the product being constructed. The customers must buy the product on the basis of the blueprint and the builders have no option during construction but to follow the blueprint exactly. If the blueprint is correct, implementation is efficient and requires only enough skill to read and follow the blueprint. If the designers are wrong or the customers cannot read blueprints, then disaster ensues. Unfortunately, failure is all too common in blueprint-style software development (Boar, 1984; Boehm, 1987; McCracken and Jackson, 1982).

The traditional or blueprint method of software development is based on several crucial presuppositions:

- That every detail about the requirements and functions of the application, no matter how complex, can be known in advance before the software is developed.
- That requirements and functions of the application will not change during development or be changed by the development itself.
- That non-technical users and managers will genuinely understand the

technical documentation produced during analysis and development.

- That users and managers will be able to communicate effectively with the analysts.
- That testing and evaluation of the software can be efficiently carried out at the end of the development.
- That development always can be partitioned into well-defined, autonomous, sequential stages.

These assumptions are the fatal flaws of the traditional software development method. They can cause many problems:

- Formal communication between user and developer is mainly in terms of computer technical notation (Mason and Carey, 1983). This is not normally the way in which users and managers think about their requirements. Users and managers may not be educationally or intellectually inclined to acquire the necessary skills to understand computer notation. It may be inefficient to expect users and managers to acquire these skills if they are only to be involved with software development a few times in their working lives. A related problem is that most people are better at judging unacceptability than at setting out positive criteria (Nozek, 1984).
- Communications between users and developers tend to be restricted to the beginning and end of the project. At the beginning, it may be too early, in terms of knowledge and relationships, to communicate effectively. At the end of the project, it may be too late to do anything or relationships may be too strained to support effective communication.
- There may be a negative attitude towards learning (Iivari, 1984) about the development after requirements analysis. Knowledge and experience (Jorgensen, 1984) is compartmentalized and being right becomes highly important. All of this inhibits effective communication and creates friction.
- Testing cannot take place until development is finished. Correcting design and implementation flaws at the end of development is more difficult and expensive after development than is correction at the earliest possible moment. Continuous early testing and user evaluation is the best way to uncover faults at the earliest opportunity.
- Any need to revise the output from preceding stages of the traditional model is likely to be considered a serious sign of failure on the part of the developers. As a consequence, revision either may be contested strongly, ignored, or performed covertly to avoid admission of failure.
- Delivery may become essentially an adversarial process. Emphasis is placed on proving that any criticism of the system is either right or wrong. There is no emphasis on correcting the points, real or perceived, that cause the criticism.

I think that if I were to encapsulate the problems that the traditional approach causes, it would be that it denies the humanity of developers and users alike. What it fundamentally ignores is that 'to err is human'.

The results of these problems are reflected in some important statistics (Tavolato and Vincena, 1984):

- Effort. Maintenance typically accounts for over 65 per cent of the effort of producing software. Requirements analysis and design account for about only 10 per cent of the total effort required in a software development project.
- Errors. Requirements deficiencies are responsible for the origin of over 55 per cent of software errors. Design flaws may account for as much as 25 per cent of software errors.
- Cost of maintenance. Requirements errors consume over 80 per cent of a typical maintenance budget. Design errors take over 10 per cent of that budget.

The implications of these statistics should be obvious. Any software development approach that does not deal effectively with improving the process of analysing and communicating user needs and requirements is a waste of time.

7.2   Prototyping in traditional development

It is in analysis and design that prototyping differs most from the conventional development approach. In the traditional, analytical approach, analysis produces a statement—in a form supposedly understood by the client—of what the software must do and how it must perform. This seems like expecting people to buy records from sheet music, instead of listening to them. Once the analysis has been agreed with the client, there is supposed to be no revision. As a consequence, any feedback after analysis and design must be suppressed, no matter how relevant the criticism.

Software producers have long employed prototypes. Dummy screens and reports (i.e. mock-up prototypes) are a normal part of eliciting customer requirements (Lee, 1979) during analysis. Prototypes are commonly used to validate algorithms (i.e. breadboard prototypes). Prototyping, when used within the traditional development approach, is even recommended as good practice (IT-STARTS, 1989a). Prototyping does not seem, however, to have gained widespread respectability within commercial software development environments. This may stem from the following:

1. The high cost of computer hardware, especially 'computer time', in the past (Martin, 1984). This notion has created a strong tradition that software developers must get it right first time, whether or not it is feasible or economical to do so.

2. The high cost of programming staff, present and future. This is reflected by concerns that prototyping is not efficient in its use of manpower or computer resources.
3. Lack of appropriate skills and software tools for prototyping in traditional programming environments.
4. Wide acceptance of the traditional view of software development, a view that does not include prototyping.

The first point does not appear to be a serious impediment to the uptake of prototyping in traditionally oriented software development environments. It is widely accepted that the real cost of computer resources has declined rapidly and is likely to continue to decline. Computer time is no longer a serious consideration in the cost of computing, although this accounting practice continues.

The second and third points are related. Programming costs are generally expected to increase in the future. The widespread introduction of highly productive software tools, such as database management systems (DBMSs) and fourth-generation languages (4GLs), can provide greater economy for prototyping than earlier generation tools could.

It is my view, and that of other authors, that prototyping is inherently more efficient than either traditional or software engineering methods in many programming environments, no matter what software tools are employed. The skills needed for successful prototyping unquestionably are, however, different from those encouraged in traditional development. Some of these skills are inherent, non-technical skills that may be difficult to acquire through training. The type of people required for prototyping is one of the topics treated later.

7.3 Conclusion

The traditional blueprint or analytical style of development became institutionalized during the 1960s, when mainframes were the dominant computer technology. The pressing commercial applications of the time were well-known and already-systematized business functions, such as accounting and order systems. Computer time was expensive and software development tools were primitive (McCracken and Jackson, 1982). The traditional method evolved to address these issues. The alternative to the analytical style of development were anarchic and expensive 'building and fixing' methods (Bates, 1989). Effective prototyping was almost impossible because computer resources were restricted and primitive.

The traditional approach to software development proved reasonably successful, particularly in well-understood or undemanding applications (Boehm *et al.*, 1984). Where applications are already well understood, static, and systematized, such as in accounting, the traditional approach is likely to continue to be reasonably successful. As computing applications become more and more complex, however, the traditional approach becomes less effective. Computing specialists who are not applications experts are less likely to be able to analyse these complex applications accurately. Even if they are expert, they still may be unable to anticipate all the pitfalls of an exceedingly complex application. Prototyping, however, appears to be an effective means of analysing even the most complex applications.

The traditional method seems so widely discredited today (Avison and Fitzgerald, 1988; Yourdon, 1989), at least in some circles, that the reader may well wonder why I have bothered to discuss the topic at all. However, the traditional method still continues to be practised widely (Boehm, 1989), either overtly or covertly, in a generally unimaginative manner. Furthermore, software engineering, the lineal successor to the traditional method, has inherited and fortified its fundamental assumptions. Prototyping, however, does not embody these fatal flaws.

The limited use of prototyping is not new in the traditional software development approach. When all is said and done, the major impediment to wider use of prototyping in traditional software development environments is likely to prove to be the conflict—real or perceived—with the traditional way of doing things. It must be remembered that computing technologists are just as subject to normal human emotions and needs as anyone else. They too suffer from 'techno-fear'. Perhaps, as the normal causative agents of techno-fear, they are less experienced at dealing with it when confronted by it themselves. Prototyping may represent a major threat to their job security, self-esteem, and professional pride. Unfortunately, there are no easy solutions to this problem.

8
Prototyping and software engineering

Software engineering has been the most sustained, respectable, and promising of initiatives to correct the problems of software development. The term software engineering appears to have been devised in the late 1960s (STARTS,1987). The legitimacy of the use of the word 'engineering' has been questioned by some (Baber, 1989); however, the term is in such widespread use as to be irretrievable. Although the term software engineering is in widespread use, there is some variation in the understanding of what constitutes software engineering. My definition is one derived from the introduction to the ACARD report (Coplin *et al.*, 1986), which states:

> Software engineering is the collection of theories, methods, skills or tools which demonstrably and repeatedly improve the productivity, quality or manageabilty of software or of the process of producing software.

To this definition, I believe that the answer to the question, 'Is software engineering the answer?' must also certainly be 'Yes'. My definition deliberately is so broad, however, that it permits almost any systematic approach to be part of software engineering. Any approach may be called software engineering, providing that it can be proven to improve any aspect of software productivity, quality, or manageability and that the improvements can be repeated by others. The question of interest really is whether the present set of theories, methods, skills, or tools do improve or are ever likely to improve the process of producing software.

As long ago as the mid-1970s, software development was claimed to be moving from a craft to an engineering discipline (Gilb, 1976). Almost 15 years later, however, there seems to be little irrefutable evidence that this transition to engineering is finished. A recent study by the Software Engineering Institute of Carnegie Mellon University (Shandle, 1989) indicates that over 70 per cent of US Department of Defense software contractors can still be classified as using 'ad hoc or, possibly, chaotic' processes for development. If the perceived lack of progress towards general acceptance and adoption of software engineering is any sign (Raghavan and Chand, 1989), it would seem to imply that software engineering has not worked at all.

8.1 Productivity

Productivity is one measure by which software engineering can be seen to work or not to work. Software productivity is the amount of satisfactory software produced for given units of resource consumed to produce it. The resource consumed is time, effort, or money (Jones, 1986). Software output is traditionally measured in terms of lines of source program delivered, a unit that has the advantage of being easily understood and well established. This practice is widely disputed as a valid measure (Boehm, 1987; Boehm and Papaccio, 1988), because it is said to provide no real indication of the rate of delivery of successful software or of its complexity. My view, however, is that any measure is likely to be better than none.

Boehm (1981 and 1987) shows that the aspects most affecting software productivity are the size of the application to be generated and the capability of the people involved in producing the software. The next most important aspect is the complexity of the application, followed by the amount of software that can be reused. This suggests that the first-order aspects of productivity are human factors. These are unlikely to be strongly related to many of the aspects that now appear to occupy the scope of software engineering (i.e. theories, methods, and tools). The potential gains from second-order factors, nevertheless, support the notion that software tools and practices can provide economically worthwhile increases in productivity. This is valid, however, only if they can be applied on a sufficiently wide scale.

Possibly the most sensible guide to the software engineering approach to improving productivity can be paraphrased from Boehm (1987):

- Get the best from people through good staff, good facilities, and good management.
- Make the steps in the software development process more efficient by using software tools, preferably well-integrated ones.
- Eliminate steps in the software development process by automating manual activities.
- Eliminate rework within the development process through computer-aided design and requirements analysis and through modern programming practices.
- Build simpler products and eliminate 'gold plating'.
- Reuse software through libraries and suitable high-level languages.

It is interesting that most of these steps seem to be involved with the human side of the software producing activity, not with the mechanistic side.

8.2 Quality

Quality is another aspect that software engineering must improve if it can be said to work. Quality, however, is a highly subjective characteristic related to the perceived excellence of something in meeting the expectations of its user or consumer. The major attributes of quality, in the software context, are as follows (Kohoutek, 1984):

- Fitness for use.
- Correctness of result.
- Reliability.

I also consider maintainability of software—in other words, the ability of a product to continue to have quality through its lifetime—to be an important aspect of quality.

In regard to quality, I have an appalling confession to make: I have not always been able to understand what quality experts are talking about. I believe that I understand what quality is and that I am oriented towards producing quality goods and services. I accept the tenet that quality from the beginning is much less costly than rework and that people should do work of the appropriate quality at every stage. Beyond those points, however, everything else seems to be labouring the blindingly obvious. Perhaps quality assurance, like software management, is more about reassuring management that they are in control of the problem than ensuring that they actually deliver quality products.

Unfortunately, the problems of measuring quality under convincing experimental conditions are almost identical to those of measuring productivity. I am therefore sceptical about the possibility of proving, beyond reasonable doubt, that software engineering can actually improve software quality. Intuitively, however, I accept that emphasis on quality, no matter what its source, is likely to improve it. Emphasis on quality, therefore, is an aspect of software engineering that I applaud.

8.3 Manageability

Manageability is concerned with the prediction and control of software production within a business context, i.e. quality, cost, and timely delivery. The following are the major attributes of software manageability:

- Accurate prediction of costs.
- Accurate prediction of time-scales.
- Accurate determination of appropriate quality.
- Delivery of software within the predicted costs.

- Delivery of software within the predicted time-scales.
- Delivery of software of appropriate quality.

In my view, software engineering is mainly about improving the manageability of software. Certainly, the appearance of manageability and control is improved by software engineering. Many software engineering tools are deeply concerned with the automatic generation of documentation, most of it for management purposes. The value of this documentation, other than satisfying demand for management-oriented documentation, does not appear proven.

Accurate prediction, of course, is the key to manageability. Boehm (1981, 1987) and other authors (W. Myers, 1989) have devised methods of predicting costs and times for large software developments in large companies. I am unable to comment on the efficacy of these methods, other than to observe that their high cost, complexity, and incomplete nature (STARTS, 1987) make them appear inappropriate for internal, custom software development, particularly in small to medium-sized organizations.

8.4 Methodologies

Methodologies, also called structured methodologies, are an integral part of contemporary software engineering. There has been a strong focus on software methodologies for many years and these have become an essential component of software engineering. Methodologies arose in the early part of the 1970s as a means of addressing the problems of generating programs. As the perception of the problems of software grew to encompass the full software life cycle, so too did the scope of methodologies grow to embrace the increased perception of the problem.

The *Concise Oxford Dictionary* (Sykes, 1976) defines a methodology as a 'Science of method; body of methods used in a particular branch of activity', while a method is a 'Special form of procedure'. The questionable use of the word methodology, rather than method, suggests the drift of the whole field. I suspect that the '-ology' has been added to impart respectability and technical flavour.

Essentially, methodologies are sets of procedures, check-lists, and documentation standards for the analysis and design of computer systems. They embody practical rules and sequences for analysing and designing software. Methodologies tend to concentrate on the graphical modelling of computer data or processes (e.g. data flow diagrams, structure diagrams, or entity-relationship models). They do not provide direct methods for eliciting user requirements, only a framework. Well-known examples of classical methodologies (Webster, 1988) are Jackson System Development (JSD), Structured Design (SD), and Structured Analysis and Design Techniques (SADT).

Methodologies provide a valuable common technical notation for professional software developers (Webster, 1988). This is especially valuable in multiple-site or multiple-organization software developments. Experienced custom software buyers increasingly expect methodologies to be used by professional software developers. Buyers may even insist upon the methodology that is used and employ the documentation as part of the contract (Coplin et al., 1986). Methodologies are undoubtedly becoming necessary in professional computing, and it is professionally difficult nowadays to defend the launching of a major software project without using an accepted methodology.

Methodologies do provide a convenient, trainable, well-documented framework for computer project management and practice. An organization adopting a methodology is, in effect, adopting a prescription for a software tradition and discipline. It is not a bad thing, given the human need to create bureaucracy, to buy in a well-considered, respectable, and ready-to-go bureaucracy than to evolve one, ad hoc. In my view, it is more important to have a methodology than it is to worry about the choice of methodologies.

Methodologies are far from perfect, however. I am unaware of any conclusive empirical evidence that methodologies improve software productivity or quality; several authors (Raghavan and Chand, 1989; Webster, 1988) share this view. Intuitively, one suspects that the quality of the software produced would be improved, but that productivity might decline because of the large amounts of paperwork required. Boar (1984) questions whether 'passive' models, a fundamental part of methodologies, are adequate for portraying applications fully. Webster (1988) amplifies concerns about the serious technical inadequacies of current methodologies.

As discussed earlier, one of the main problems in custom software development is finding out what users want and need. The other problem is software maintenance. Methodologies do not appear to offer any particular insight into either of these problems, nor do they seem an effective means of communicating with average users and managers (Mason and Carey, 1983; Parbst, 1984). The other problem is that there are no standards for the highly diverse range of available methodologies (Webster, 1988). As a consequence, there is a danger of adopting and investing in a methodology that will become obsolete or one that is vulnerable to arbitrary price manipulation by its supplier.

In general, methodologies would appear to add considerably to computing overheads and to retard development, possibly without conferring any direct benefits. They are not likely to be of much benefit when working with users or non-technical management. On the other hand, they do provide a well-accepted framework for technically oriented development and communication. The framework is one for which replacement staff can be found or trained. In their indirect benefits, methodologies probably do improve the survivability of the software produced and, thus, contribute to its long-term success. Whether this is cost effective or not is a question I cannot answer. It is disturbing, however, that methodologies may not be technically adequate for their intended purpose (Webster, 1988).

The question of whether small and medium-sized organizations engaged in custom software should adopt methodologies is not an easy one to answer. In these types of organizations, the large investment required for training and, possibly, licences to use the methodology are daunting. Typically, an organization can expect to spend 2–4 weeks training per person initially and at least a week a year thereafter. This is a major investment for many organizations, especially when the benefits, in terms of productivity or quality, cannot be quantified. On the other hand, continuity of the computing organization must be of prime importance. If methodologies provide that, at least, then they almost certainly are worth using.

8.5 Problems in software engineering

In spite of its worthy goals, software engineering seems to be a long way from achieving unequivocal success (Bates, 1989) or universal acceptance. Software engineering does not appear to offer any effective means of improving the translation of user needs and requirements into working software. More seriously, software engineering, especially computer-aided software engineering (CASE), may even hamper the user–developer interface by inserting thicker and more turgid layers of technology and bureaucracy. I fear that software engineering may amplify many of the 'anti-people' aspects of computing practice, to the detriment of users and businesses. I have a concern, as well, that software engineering tends to treat implementation as a trivial activity of software development. Software still needs to be written and delivered; design alone is not enough.

The traditional, analytical method of software development is based on fallacious presuppositions. These have been inherited by software engineering in a slightly mutated form:

- That everything can be known in advance, or can be discovered during analysis, about application needs and requirements (Fischer, 1989).
- That needs and requirements will not change faster than development or will not be changed by the development process itself.
- That the users genuinely understood the documentation and diagrams presented to them by software engineers.
- That testing and evaluation should be left until after design and implementation is completed.

Another problem is that the current practice of software engineering is heavily dependent on methodologies. Methodologies, however, may be technically inadequate or of doubtful value (Webster, 1988).

Software engineering does not appear particularly appropriate for small and medium-sized organizations that produce routine custom business soft-ware. The current thrust of software engineering is being driven by the manage-ment needs of organizations that produce very large and complex software systems. These often technically challenging systems may have life-critical or high reliability requirements. These very large systems may involve hun-dreds of man-years of development work, very large budgets, and hundreds of staff (STARTS, 1987). Typically, however, the problems addressed at the leading edge of software engineering are not those of the average commer-cial computer operation. For the average commercial operation, a six man-month long software development may be a large one. It may have less than half a dozen software developers and a very limited budget. It is hardly sur-prising if software engineering does not meet the needs of the average com-mercial software developer in this environment.

8.6   Computer-aided software engineering

Computer-aided software engineering is one of the most prominent areas of software engineering. CASE is primarily the computer automation of methodologies (Butler Cox, 1988), and some CASE products even manage to support several methodologies. CASE tools have been called the 'power tools' (Martin and Hershey, 1984) of software development.

CASE products (STARTS, 1987) emphasize the elimination of manual work in producing analysis and design documentation and the ease of gen-erating new editions of documentation. Consistency of design methods, notation, and automatic cross-checking are also often cited as benefits. CASE technology includes computer-aided design (CAD), generation of code for specifications (usually only partial), graphics, prototyping, and even a dollop of artificial intelligence (Martin and Hershey, 1984). Some CASE products claim to offer a full set of software development tools for addressing the entire software life cycle.

It is hardly surprising that software engineering emphasis has settled on CASE, given the computer industry's propensity for seeking all-encompassing solutions. What is driving the move towards CASE? The major factors appear to be the following:

- CASE is being stimulated by defence establishments such as the Depart-ment of Defense in the US, the Ministry of Defence in the UK, and NATO. Some prominent defence-led initiatives that seem to have stimu-lated interest in CASE are ADA programming support environments (APSE), common APSE interface standards (CAIS), and portable common tool environments (PCTE).
- CASE offers a means for large (i.e. projects taking between 20 and 200 man-years) software development buyers, primarily in the defence and aerospace industries, to deal uniformly with software producers and

suppliers. CASE even offers the possibility of managing multi-sourced software development within a single project.

- Company management demands for greater software productivity or reduction of computing costs. CASE products promise to solve all the problems of desperate software development managers.
- The need to attract and retain development staff members by providing them with modern programming environments and experience. CASE products are a major focus of the software development field. Experience in CASE aids the employability of computer personnel.
- CASE may appeal to the worst side of software developers' natures. CASE particularly helps developers avoid the human issues of software development and provides automated tools for the technical intimidation of users.
- Possibly the strongest pressure for adopting CASE is the commercial interest and marketing 'hype' of software tool and CASE suppliers.

The perceived difficulties of CASE, particularly for small and medium-sized companies with an existing base of software, are manifold:

- There is a lack of impartial evidence about the demonstrable benefits of adopting CASE tools (Guest, 1989). Indeed, there is evidence that some CASE tools reduce productivity (Falk, 1989).
- The subject is highly complex and technical. Even a superficial evaluation could take several man-years effort (STARTS, 1987).
- The cost of acquiring CASE technology is high. Substantial hardware investment in workstations is usually required, and payback may take 10 years (Butler Cox, 1988). The typical cost of supplying CASE to a developer may exceed his salary costs for one year. Unit costs may not drop appreciably with volume. Infrastructural and support costs may be much higher than expected (Jones, 1986). For example, associated training and consultancy needs could raise total CASE costs by as much as 50 per cent (Samish, 1989).
- Most software operations suffer more from the burden of maintaining existing software than from the demands of developing new software. Although there are products specifically designed for reverse engineering (Falk, 1989), these are not a part of most CASE products. Consequently, CASE does not effectively address one of the most pressing software problems.
- Lack of standards for CASE tools increases the risk of making a bad or prematurely obsolete investment. It also encourages lack of integration among diverse CASE tools.
- Existing CASE products are immature, performance is poor, and function is incomplete (Butler Cox, 1988; Webster, 1988). The technical problems facing the next generation of CASE tools are said to be great (Falk, 1989).

- Most seriously from the normal business programming viewpoint, CASE products do not address the problem of extracting the needs and requirements of users, nor do they really address the problems of software maintenance. The sheer volume, complexity, and highly technical nature of CASE (Butler Cox, 1988) is likely to alienate typical users even further from software developers than the traditional, analytical approach.

My conclusion is that CASE sets out to automate methodologies that are themselves of unproven or even dubious value (Webster, 1988). The productivity gains of CASE come largely from automating the tedious and voluminous documentation required by methodologies. Far from solving the problems of software development, even more problems are likely to be generated by the introduction of aggressively marketed but technically complex and immature CASE products. Any organization that commits itself to CASE should do so with full knowledge of the problems, the limitations, and the likely magnitude of the investment.

Large organizations may find CASE of value in automating their software bureaucracy. Companies of any size working within the defence and aerospace sectors may find CASE essential for gaining business. Small and medium-sized organizations engaged in conventional, customized business software development, however, are unlikely to find CASE of as much benefit. On the contrary, they are likely to find CASE an expensive and disruptive disappointment. Some of the problems I perceive with the present style of software engineering for custom software producers in small and medium-sized organizations are:

- Unproven effectiveness.
- High cost and long payback.
- Possible slower development speed and 'paralysis by design'.
- Increasing the technology gap between designers and users.
- Risk of adopting unproven technology.
- Risk of adopting non-standard technology.
- Difficulty of 'reverse-engineering' existing software.

8.7 Formal methods

Mathematically based formal methods (STARTS, 1987), such as HOS, OBJ, Z, and VDM are proposed as a software engineering solution that could provide a breakthrough in the quality of software (Ince, 1988; Martin 1984). Formal methods may be capable of producing mathematically provable code, but they avoid totally the major problem of custom software development, namely the elicitation of user requirements (Avison and Fitzgerald, 1988). If a problem can be expressed in a mathematical notation, then it already has had these requirements extracted from the users (Haughton, 1989).

Formal methods unfortunately cannot eliminate conceptual programming errors or gross misconceptions about the organization for which they are being employed. Most formal methods are still experimental, require much training in their use (Webster, 1988), and appear to demand considerable intellectual ability. Their run-time efficiency, if they can be executed at all, is low (Bates, 1989). I believe that the value of formal methods is highly limited in conventional commercial applications and is likely to remain so for a long time.

8.8 Conclusion

The current approach of software engineering sometimes reminds me of the military treatment given to the Western Front in the First World War. The generals and their staff theoreticians slid their pointers from point A to point B. They ignored the realities of weather, terrain, machine guns, or condition of their troops. The infantry were ordered to make carefully planned frontal assaults, in spite of the amply demonstrated lack of success of this form of attack throughout the war. When the attacks failed, so strong was the faith in the frontal attack that the corrective action was to make discipline more rigid and the frontal attacks even bigger. This stupidity and abject incompetence resulted in repeated failure and terrible waste. 'Lions led by asses': it may prove a fitting epitaph for software engineering too.

In spite of the much-touted advances of software engineering, the fundamental problems of software development remain. Computing generally fails to satisfy its users and the organizations that pay for it and maintenance critical mass still occurs. The inadequacy of software engineering may be that, as practised, it does not seriously address the main problem of producing software: that of deriving accurate requirements. Worse still, software engineering remedies may not prove harmless to organizations that adopt them. Fischer (1989) sums up the current trend of software engineering neatly, 'the implementation disasters of the 1960s will be succeeded by the design disasters of the 1980s'.

Prototyping has become one of the major issues of software engineering (Hekmatpour and Ince, 1986). There is considerable controversy, however, about the role of prototyping within the subject. Views seem to range from prototyping being contrary to everything for which software engineering stands, to prototyping being an essential component of software engineering. There seems little doubt that prototyping could be accommodated within the broad definition of software engineering. Computer-aided software engineering tools can almost certainly be developed or modified to prototype efficiently (Luqi and Berzins, 1988). Prototyping may well be able to help software engineering address the problem of eliciting user needs and requirements. An effective combination of the rigour of software engineering with the human-oriented philosophy of prototyping is a truly exciting prospect.

Part Three
Adoption of prototyping

The introduction of prototyping into an organization is similar to technology transfer problems of any sort. It is important to remember, however, that prototyping is not a technology. Properly moulded skills, attitudes, and expectations are essential for all involved in the prototyping process—prototypers, users, and management. One might better categorize the necessary process of transfer as one of education and attitude change.

I would, in general, advise that computing management should insulate its users and non-technical management from purely technical computing issues as much as possible. This insulation is not intended to deprive these people of technical knowledge, but rather to spare their sensibilities and patience for issues that will require their intervention. The adoption of prototyping, however, is difficult to treat as a purely internal computing issue. It is a matter in which general participation is beneficial.

The major issue of adopting prototyping is less one of which software tool to use, but rather of which people to use. Prototyping is bound to be more effective if users have an understanding of the aims, processes, and goals of prototyping. They should also be educated about what they can reasonably expect from prototyping. The skill and personal abilities of the technical staff are the key to success in prototyping. Finally, prototyping requires strong and flexible management. The issue of people and prototyping is sufficiently important that I have devoted a chapter in this section to the subject.

9
Strategies for adopting prototyping

Almost invariably, the transfer of anything really new into an organization is a long and hard battle, sometimes taking as much as a decade to complete. There usually must be a 'champion' who single-mindedly instigates and leads the adoption process. These people are either champions because it is their job to do so or because they particularly believe in what they are doing. The latter type of prototyping champion is particularly advised to examine his or her motives carefully before starting and to attempt to maintain an objective viewpoint at all times.

Once the initial decision has been made to attempt to introduce prototyping into an organization, at whatever level, careful re-evaluation is still needed to ensure that the approach is genuinely appropriate to the organization. If further evaluation proves favourable, then adoption should be planned carefully. Planning is needed to avoid unnecessary disruption to the software development operation and to ensure that the education and attitude formation campaign has reached all concerned.

One of the most important aspects of planning for technology transfer should be for withdrawal if transfer proves unsuccessful. One of the comforting aspects about prototyping adoption is that it need not be an all-or-nothing exercise. The adoption of prototyping need not involve major upfront capital or staff investment, but can be undertaken incrementally and embedded within traditional operations. If it does not work, it should be possible to retreat from prototyping without major loss. My advice to those championing prototyping is to avoid irretrievable commitment—financial, technical, or emotional—until it is certain that the system will work within the host organization.

9.1   Prototyping transfer

Galitz (1980) and Raghavan and Chand (1989) provide useful advice for the introduction of new technology. This can be rephrased for a prototyping champion as follows:

- Develop an aura of success, power, legitimacy, and credibility. Although this may not seem the most honourable way of encouraging the adoption of prototyping, it must be remembered that many people are not greatly driven by rational technical issues. A virtuoso display of the technical issues may only serve to confuse them. The only thing worse would be a public battle with fellow technologists.
- Encourage users to foster positive attitudes about the change to prototyping. In particular, play on the theme that prototyping puts the users in charge. The positive attitude of users should encourage their management to decide in favour of prototyping. Reduction of users' 'technophobia' will make prototyping more efficient once it has been adopted.
- Keep in step with user and management commitment to prototyping. Watch carefully for any signs of resistance. Remember that most people are adverse to change. Move in small steps to reduce the appearance of radical change. Wait for 'grass-roots' enthusiasm to appear and then exploit it rapidly when it arises.
- Propose to implement changes in areas that will show the greatest benefits first. Typically, these will be systems with the most frequent usage or for which there is the greatest demand. Make certain that the initial system will succeed, but that it also will show early and quantifiable benefits.
- Mould reasonable expectations of users and management. It is important that all concerned are enthusiastic about the adoption of prototyping. This enthusiasm must, however, be tempered with reality. This will not only foster the adoption of prototyping, it also will make prototyping more successful if it is adopted.
- Define clear objectives and resource needs for adoption. Make sure you achieve your objectives on time and within budget. Make sure that the people who matter in your organization know that you have performed to target.
- Expect slow, difficult, and gradual adoption. Technology transfer can take 10–20 years. Resistance to prototyping is more likely to be encountered from computer technologists than from users and non-technical management.

9.2   Preliminary evaluation

The champion must be absolutely certain that the prototyping approach is genuinely feasible, beneficial, and psychologically amenable to the adopting organization before proceeding. The 'no-go' areas for prototyping were laid out in Chapter 6. If you work in one of these areas, then a better approach is to look for opportunities to try partial, throw-away prototypes. You might also attempt to propose prototyping purely as a means of eliciting user requirements or developing human–computer interfaces (HCIs).

Before categorically accepting or rejecting prototyping, the champion should first take a leaf out of the prototyping book; in other words, prototype prototyping. Here are the basic steps:

- Pick a relatively simple project. Ensure that it is typical of the organization.
- Use your best staff for prototypers. Ensure they are committed to the success of the experiment.
- Make no special investment in software tools for prototyping. Employ tools that are familiar to the prototypers.
- Identify your users carefully. Ensure they have time allocated formally for the experiment and are acquainted with the goals and processes of the prototyping approach.
- Keep a detailed and accurate diary of the experiment. Instrument the experiment with productivity, quality and cost measurements from the beginning. Include subjective observations about attitudes and morale.
- Quantify the results of the experiment in terms of cost, productivity, quality and user satisfaction. Use the simplest productivity measures your organization will accept. Opinion polls of those involved in the experiment should be a satisfactory way of quantifying user satisfaction. Polls are relatively easy to devise and inexpensive to carry out. It will be particularly instructive to carry out polls at several points in the experiment.
- Communicate the results of your experiment to those you think should know about them. Do not wait until the experiment is finished to do so. This will give an opportunity to build or reduce expectations about the final results. Remember that most people hate surprises in business.

When evaluating the result of the experiment, be sceptical. Remember that the Hawthorne Effect will be in effect and that everyone involved will be fresh and eager. If the experience with prototyping gives adequate confidence, however, then the champion should plan for proposing formal adoption. If the experiment with prototyping does not work in the particular environment, then drop it and cut your losses. No large-scale commitment to prototyping, either financial or emotional, should be made that will make backing out disastrous. This is one of the main reasons for employing conventional software tools for prototyping, especially at the beginning. Adopting prototyping should not be made an irreversible process or a test of wills.

9.3 Management support

The champion of prototyping will certainly need to seek the understanding and support of both top and middle management on a wide basis. This can only be achieved by effective communication of the benefits of prototyping. In a few cases, prototyping champions may have sufficient authority to introduce prototyping without the approval of their peers and superiors. Even here, user management should be informed since their cooperation is vital and the champions will still need to enlist the support of their own managers.

The prototyping benefits that are likely to attract management attention most are the following:

- Improved productivity or cost effectiveness. Although this is the strongest argument that can be employed, it may prove dangerous unless it is certain that prototyping will actually be able to lower computing costs within the organization.
- Improved flexibility and speed of software development. This can be presented as improving the competitive ability of the organization. This may be a very effective argument in fast-moving organizations.
- Competitors. Many organizations are strongly driven by what other organizations are doing, particularly their competitors. If your competitors are using prototyping effectively, you may need very little further evidence to persuade some organizations. If they are not using prototyping, then it may be productive to emphasize the competitive ability that prototyping could give.
- Improved user involvement and satisfaction. This can be presented as being likely to result in higher-quality software, at least from the users' point of view. Increased user satisfaction may not be an effective approach in some organizations: it may be perceived as being too 'soft'.
- Early software evaluation and use. Some managers may be intrigued by the prospect of early and realistic evaluation of software, particularly if this permits them to cancel unpromising developments before they start to cost too much.

A good method of ensuring adequate coverage of influence is to create a list of managers you think you should contact. Decide why and how they should be approached. Make sure particularly that you include people who are likely to be antagonistic to your proposal. Finally, make sure that you do contact all of these people. Use both formal and informal channels of communication and appeal to reach them.

Informal means of communication can be very important as a means of sustaining your supporters and softening your antagonists before formal proposals are attempted. Often, your supporters will need continual assurances that 'everything is going to go all right' and see that you can keep a straight face while you are saying it. Your antagonists will normally air their arguments against you, if you give them half a chance to do so. This gives you advance warning of their arguments. Better still, it is a private opportunity for immediate resolution or diminution of their antagonism.

9.4 Technical issues

Before moving to seek formal adoption of prototyping, it is wise to have a firm view on whether or not your operation should proceed with the more radical form of prototyping, evolutionary prototyping. You should be very sure of your ground before you do propose evolutionary prototyping. Ensure especially that you will not encounter resistance from technicians within your organization. They are the ones most likely to feel threatened by it. A public battle within the computing operation will not give general confidence in any form of prototyping.

Be prepared to compromise with the existing software development approach in the organization. Throw-away prototyping is capable of coexisting with and assisting both the traditional software development and software engineering approaches without difficulty. Throw-away prototyping can be presented simply as being a part of the elicitation of needs and requirements from users. Evolutionary prototyping is a radical step, however, and it may prove difficult to defend. At present, it does not fall within the boundaries of the best practice of conservative software development (IT-STARTS, 1989a).

One of the main attractions of evolutionary prototyping, however, is the possibility of eliminating some of the software development bureaucracy. If prototyping can be controlled, then significant productivity gains and cost reductions could be achieved by eliminating management overheads. In some organizations, however, evolutionary prototyping may be so culturally alien or perceived as so anti-management as to have no chance of succeeding. It is likely that methods, literature, and traditions will have to form around the practice of evolutionary prototyping before it will become generally acceptable practice.

Another part of the adoption strategy should be how to treat and maintain previous software investment. The best advice here is to heed the old saying, 'If it ain't broke, don't fix it.' This means that your new prototype-developed software will have to coexist with old software. Here, old software may best be treated as 'black boxes' with well-defined interfaces. The old software is repaired when necessary, but not enhanced, and it is replaced only when genuinely necessary. New software grows around the framework of the old software. There is bound to be some inefficiency in this approach, but this is likely to be preferable to going to your management with a scheme to replace all the software in the organization.

Your adoption strategy should embody some ideas of how you will organize and manage prototyping within your computing facility. This theme is elaborated in the next section. Boar (1984) makes a strong case for a prototyping centre, which is a useful idea, especially if your organization already has computing centres for data or other functions. For project-oriented companies, proposing prototyping project teams may be a more appropriate approach. Other considerations may be the employment of consultants and what will happen to the prototypers after the prototype is finished.

9.5 Prototyping tools and adoption

There is considerable discussion in this book and in the literature about prototyping tools. The message of this book, however, is that lack of specialized software tools need not be an impediment to prototyping. Prototyping will be better with good tools, of course, but poor tools may give better results with prototyping than the same tools used with any other development approach. Introducing new tools during an initial essay into prototyping is not advisable. If you have a suitable database management system available, you may need look no further for prototyping tools for most applications.

The prototyping tool issue may have its greatest benefit as a 'red herring'. If tools can be made an issue with the computer technologists within the organization, then these technologists may become so preoccupied with evaluation and discussion of tools as to let the greater issues pass by. In this case, however, it is important that contention does not spill over out of the computing operation or actually impede adoption. Bypassing the computer operation simply to avoid conflict will not, however, prove wise in the long run. It is essential that the prototyping champion wins the hearts and minds of the technologists as well as those of management and the users.

9.6 Conclusion

Adopting prototyping is likely to prove as much a political issue as a technical one. Those who champion its adoption should take heed of this. The adoption of prototyping is a decision that should not be confined to the computing operation. Involvement of users and management in the decision to adopt this approach is essential, especially if they are expected to participate in prototype development. Since prototyping essentially is a user-oriented approach, however, enlisting the support of users and non-technical managers should prove relatively easy. Technical issues are unlikely to arise within this area.

The greatest opposition to adopting prototyping in an organization is likely to come from others engaged in computing. Prototyping may be perceived as a serious threat to the computing status quo. Contention is likely to take place over apparently technical issues. Without consensus of opinion in favour of prototyping within the computing operation, adoption could prove to be an unproductive exercise. Consequently, the issues, both technical and political, must be addressed authoritatively and sensitively.

10

Prototyping and people

Prototyping is an approach to carrying out software development, not a detailed prescription. Prototyping does not even necessarily require any capital investment or even any special training. Probably the most important 'tool' for prototyping is simply having the correct attitude. This makes the adoption of prototyping an act that is simultaneously both simple and difficult. From an adoption viewpoint, the most serious consideration may be whether the organization has people of the appropriate attitude, skill, and personality to carry out prototyping successfully. Without the right people, prototyping is likely to fail.

10.1 Attitude

The correct attitude must be found in all three classes of 'player' involved in prototype development: prototyper, user, and manager. Using unsuitable people for prototyping is likely to lead to even worse results than using the traditional development approach. The main reasons for this danger are the following:

- Users and software developers must interact more often and more successfully than in the traditional approach. The opportunities for friction are thus much greater and the consequences more serious.
- The expertise of developers, users, and managers is on public show. Lack of expertise will be quickly revealed in situations where it may prove difficult to 'save face'.
- Prototyping depends on rapid and genuine results from the developer. This requires considerable dedication and a great deal of technical skill.
- Prototyping generally implies the use of smaller development teams with a wider range of skills than required in traditional development.

There is a great need for political awareness in all those involved in proto-typing. Managers particularly must be able quickly and smoothly to resolve the problems that the users and developers cannot.

10.2 Prototyping and prototypers

The most important prerequisite for prototypers (i.e. prototype developers) is an appropriate frame of mind and adequate technical skill. The earlier background chapter about people discussed the theme that many of those involved in computing have or develop personality traits that make them poorly suited for prototyping. It seems likely that finding and retaining effective prototype development staff may prove one of the major problems of and limitations to prototyping.

The personal qualities required in a good prototyper are formidable, especially considering the psychological profiles of many programmers (Couger and Zawacki, 1980). All of the qualities required for prototyping are unlikely to be found in a highly developed form in a single individual. No prototyper, however, should be seriously deficient in any of these qualities. These personal qualities, in alphabetical order, are as follows:

- Communications skill. The ability to communicate well, particularly to non-computing management, is an asset in prototyping. Good commu-nication in the opposite direction, i.e. listening, is obviously highly important. Plenty of practice and advice can improve communications skills greatly.
- Flexibility. Prototyping is a way of dealing with change and uncertainty. There is little room for the dogmatic hypothesis in prototyping, except perhaps as a temporary ruse to 'unstick' uncommunicative users. Flexi-bility is largely an inherent skill and one commonly found in programmers.
- Motivation and stamina. Most programmers have unusually high moti-vation (Couger and Zawacki, 1980). Prototypers, however, are bound to experience frequent setbacks in their work; it is often necessary to scrap days of work and good ideas. Prototypers may work long hours to over-come these setbacks. During prototype development, physical and mental fatigue can become a genuine problem. A high degree of motivation is needed to see the job through to the end. Managers can help through financial incentives, adroit encouragement, and by not letting their staff work themselves to exhaustion.
- Patience. Prototyping can have its tedious moments, as well as exciting ones. Often, the prototyper will just have to sit and wait until users are ready to participate. Patience also is needed during some of the more infuriating moments with incredibly complacent, ignorant, and even malignant users. I personally try to repeat the mantra 'suffer fools gladly' during some of these moments. Patience with users is not one of the more notable features of most programmers.

- Personability. Prototyping is most certain to fail if the prototyper does not get along with the users. If the prototyper is a likeable, non-threatening, humble sort of person, so much the better. This is a quality that is unlikely to be learned easily. Personability is not essential to good programming, but nor is it a hindrance.
- Interpersonal skill. Prototypers will often be acting as an agent of unwanted change. While the prototyper generally should be honest and open, there are times when being 'economical with the truth' may be advisable. Some people seem to be born with considerable interpersonal skill, others acquire it with age and experience; some programmers have it and others do not. The best advice I can give to fellow lackers of this skill is to try to discuss the weather a lot.
- Sympathy with the users. A prototyper without a genuine degree of understanding and tolerance of user motivation will find it difficult to sustain the patience and motivation required for successful prototyping. Those who have been in the position of user are likely to have greater sympathy than those who have never acted in this capacity. This is why recruitment of prototypers from the 'ranks' is always worth considering. Programmers otherwise are notoriously lacking in sympathy for users.
- Technical competence. The prototyper must be able to create the prototype rapidly. This requires a high level of programming skill and a good knowledge of the software tools being employed. Prototypers also need to know when they are out of their depth. They should not be afraid to tell users that they do not know an answer, but that they will find out. Technical competence can be improved through training and education, but an inherent talent for programming may be essential.

Fortunately, prototyping may represent a considerable streamlining of the software development operation. From a programmer's point of view, prototyping may be a release from the bureaucracy of rigid design and analysis procedures and an enhancement of the enjoyable aspects of programming. Prototyping may be seen as an opportunity for advancement since prototypers really are business analyst programmers (Livesey, 1984).

Some of the less positive effects on software development staff that may arise from adopting prototyping are the following:

- A new intake of staff may be needed. It may be felt that development staff may be insufficiently skilled, too occupied with existing software maintenance, or too resistant to the uptake of prototyping. Recruitment of new staff, temporary or permanent, may be necessary. This, in turn, may disrupt or alienate existing staff even more.
- Staff attrition. Some software developers may be sufficiently unhappy about the introduction of prototyping to leave the organization. The possibility of significant and serious attrition of development staff should be considered before adopting prototyping.

- Training. Formal training courses typically cost 2–4 staff salary weeks per week of training. Some formal orientation in the techniques and management of prototyping may be felt to be necessary; a few days should be sufficient, however. Several weeks training could be required if new programming tools are adopted.
- Familiarization. These are the non-training costs, mainly loss of productivity, associated with introducing prototyping into a new environment. Good and willing programmers should require only a brief familiarization period.

10.3 Prototyping and software managers

For the programmer turned software manager prototyping may offer an opportunity to return to many of the pleasurable aspects of programming. Managing prototyping gives a lot more feedback and more immediate results than conventional software development. There should be less paperwork and more opportunity for involvement in development issues. Progress is easier to monitor and the results are more tangible than in traditional project management (Weinberg, 1971).

For the non-technical software manager, prototyping may appear worrying because of the need for greater flexibility and the difficulty of establishing fixed targets. On the other hand, it should be easier to monitor real, as opposed to paper, progress. There is absolutely nothing to prevent software managers from sitting down with the users and prototypers and reviewing progress with them and then evaluating the prototype themselves. If they do, there is little chance that non-technical managers will be hoodwinked badly.

The qualities needed by prototype managers are all the ones required by any good managers. Particular emphasis, however, is needed on the following:

- Interpersonal skills. Because frequent contact with users is needed, often under difficult circumstances, even the best prototypers may occasionally antagonize the users. Early perception of interpersonal problems and the ability to smooth them down are needed by prototyping managers.
- Political skills. Politics is the art of gaining status and influence within the organization. The interpersonal skills necessary to soothe an angry user are not alone sufficient. Prototyping managers are often highly visible political trouble-shooters. They must also be able to manoeuvre successfully among their own peers and higher management and survive the experience.
- Man-management skills. Because good prototyping staff are valuable, it is important that managers retain them and keep them working happily. Good man-management is needed to maintain momentum during the slow phases of development and to ensure that the developers receive the

rapid feedback that they have come to expect. Developers also have to have their noses kept to the grindstone, in the nicest possible way.

- Flexibility and resolve. Prototyping managers must be prepared to change their way of working and of presenting themselves within the company. Once within the prototype development, a reasonable amount of flexibility is needed to cope with the fluid nature of prototype development. Flexibility must be tempered with an equal amount of resolve to get the job done, in spite of the many obstacles, diversions, and opportunities that may appear.
- Good judgment. Prototyping managers will be expected to achieve balance between the needs of the organization and the needs of the users. They will not be able to fall back on tradition for their solutions. They will also be expected to arbitrate between what is technically reasonable and the demands of the organization and the users. Finally, they need to be able to judge, either through technical knowledge or personal intuition, whether or not their prototypers are deceiving them.
- Technically knowledgeable. Prototyping managers must be able to provide active and decisive technical leadership. Programmers generally respond most willingly to managers who have a genuine appreciation of what they do and how they do it. Managers will also benefit from a strong knowledge of the application.

The following are some of the difficulties that managers may encounter with prototyping:

- Prototyping is more about achieving results than about producing the appearance of management. This may be a serious difficulty to both traditional managers and to organizations that take reporting more seriously than progress and planning more seriously than reality.
- Prototyping could reduce development staff populations. This in turn could cause a loss in income potential, career enhancement, and self-esteem for managers. This may be a problem in organizations in which salary and promotion prospects are guided primarily by the size of staff managed, rather than by the results achieved.
- Managers who are not 'on top of their jobs', either in terms of technical or political competence, are likely to find prototyping exposing their weaknesses quickly and publicly.

10.4 Prototyping and users

The users are the 'poor bloody infantry' of computing. Fear and anxiety were presented earlier as the great motivators of computing users. Prototyping is a great helper in reducing user fear and anxiety. Prototyping puts users directly in the software development loop, and this should help users to feel more in control of the software that may affect them profoundly.

Knowledge and familiarity of users is the key to willing and rapid acceptance of computing (Coplin *et al.*, 1986). Prototyping is an excellent way of learning about computing (Bates, 1989). User enjoyment and satisfaction is an important, but underestimated (King, 1983), aspect in their acceptance of software. Prototyping is an effective and inexpensive means of providing enjoyment and satisfaction for users, as well as software developers.

Just as not all programmers and software managers are suited for prototyping, neither are all users suitable to participate in prototyping. Careful user selection is just as important as selecting the rest of the prototyping team. Some of the qualities of a good user are as follows:

- Technical competence and scope; the user should provide much of the application view of the prototype. This view should not be parochial, otherwise the prototype will be flawed and more iterations will be required.
- Good interpersonal skills are as necessary for the user as for everyone else involved in the prototype. Users with an obvious chip on their shoulders or who refuse to communicate are likely to foil the best prototyper.
- A high degree of confidence is needed by the users. Users who are overwhelmed or awed by the developers are not likely to make much of a contribution. The users may need to stand up to the prototypers and make their voices heard.

Prototyping cannot proceed successfully without active user participation. Evaluation of users is an important aspect of adoption.

10.5 Prototyping and non-computing management

General or non-computing management is too often inclined to leave software development to the 'peons', and only become involved when there is a crisis or when funding is requested. Software, however, is becoming too important for management to ignore or to limit their interest to the 'bottom line'. Management should take an active and a positive role in software development. If they do not, they are contributing significantly to the possibility of failure.

Contribution from management throughout prototyping is valuable to ensure that software development is moving along a course that is most beneficial to the business. Users quite rightly take a focused view that the software should do what they need it to do for their jobs. Good prototype developers should carry out the wishes of the users without attempting to impose themselves to the point of friction. This highly focused view, however, may not necessarily be what the whole organization needs. Only management can contribute a wider organizational view to the software. Furthermore, without management participation, opportunities to change the way in which users work or to link functions outside the local knowledge of users could be missed.

The following are some of the benefits of involving general management in prototyping:

- Prototyping is easier for non-technical managers to understand and criticize, and therefore helps them contribute to the software being developed. Continuous assessment by managers should help defuse potential crises or confrontations.
- Prototyping gives management confidence that something tangible is being produced from the expenditure that they may have authorized or for which they are responsible.
- Prototyping gives management an opportunity to see their staff—the users—interacting with the software and its developers. The involvement of managers in prototyping will convey the seriousness of the software development to the users.
- Prototyping gives management an opportunity to contribute their experience, ideas, and needs to the development. This also diffuses the 'ownership' of the software to high levels within the organization.
- Prototyping gives competent software developers and managers an opportunity to show their ability and to enhance their relations with management. Successful prototyping can help build trust between general management and computing management.

It is a very serious mistake to omit general management from the prototyping process. The earlier their contribution is made, the fewer problems the development team will have at the end of the project. Adoption of prototyping may prove risky if full involvement of management cannot be secured.

10.6 Education

Prototyping puts emphasis on the skills and competence of all involved. It is often assumed that anyone who calls himself or herself a 'programmer' must be technically competent. On the contrary, the pressure to continue maintaining existing software and to produce new software means that just about anyone can get a job as a programmer (Boehm, 1988). It is necessary seriously to consider whether the staff within the organization have sufficient skill and educational background to sustain the prototyping approach. Even where computing staff have genuine competence and background, it cannot be assumed that this competence will necessarily remain current in a rapidly changing field. Continued education and training are needed.

It cannot be taken for granted, either, that an academic degree in computing is necessarily a guarantee of good applications development skills. The lack of established educational traditions for software producers (Coplin et al., 1986) means that the competence of computer science graduates cannot be taken for granted. On the contrary, academic attitudes may be a serious impediment (Barron and Curnow, 1979) to the effective use of technology. A computer science degree is only likely to mean that recipients know a third-generation computer language well and have their heads stuffed full of technical facts that may be irrelevant to 'real' software development.

Organizations must educate their technical staff. Those who engage in prototyping have an even stronger requirement to do so. Even the most competent computer technologists require a regular amount of:

• General technological education.
• General business education and training.
• Specific education in the business of the organization.
• Specific training in the tools and techniques employed in their organization.

There is little point in an organization lavishing education and training on its computer staff, however, if they have to operate in the company of ignorant users and management. Organizations must also ensure that their other staff, especially management, have a general appreciation of computing technology and have adequate training in the computer tools that they employ in their jobs.

10.7   Conclusion

Software is now much too important for organizations to leave its development in the hands of programmers. The software developer's legitimate role should be that of translating user needs and requirements, within the context of the needs and requirements of the host organization, into software. Too often, users and general management abdicate their proper responsibilities to programming staff. Prototyping places, quite properly, a much greater burden and responsibility on users and non-computing management for the production of their software than either the traditional or software engineering approaches. Adoption must seriously address this issue.

Prototyping requires a high level of genuine competence in several areas from all those engaged in the process. Not only must the prototyping team be enthusiastic and able to interact well on a personal level, but all must be competent in their area of responsibility. This is not an easy combination to find, but once it is found,the effects can be impressive. Remember that different levels of skill can vary the amount of software that is produced by as much as a factor of 10: this is the difference between someone who can run a 4 minute mile and someone who can run a mile in 40 minutes. Outstanding people working in well-managed harmony are the only magic ingredients I know of for software development. If an organization does not have the right people, then it should not consider prototyping a suitable software development approach.

11
Adoption: prototyping tools

The selection of prototyping tools is bound to take up a considerable part of any discussion about adopting prototyping. This is because of the difficulty of prescribing the way to achieve the correct attitude for prototyping and because of the computing industry's cultural obsession with tools. Discussion of tool requirements, fortunately, has the benefit of exposing many of the human issues of adopting prototyping.

The main requirements of software tools for prototyping are that they should support the following:

- Business effectiveness.
- Functionality.
- Rapid development.
- 'Deliverability'.
- Maintainability.

11.1 Business effective prototyping tools

Prototyping can vitally affect organizations into which it is introduced. The consequences of adopting poorly supported prototyping tools or, worse still, of having to discontinue their use could be severe. Consequently, prototyping tools that are outside the risk-limits the organization would consider for any other vital business functions (e.g. choice of bank) should not be employed. Even perceived risk about prototyping tools may become known and damage the effectiveness of all aspects of prototyping.

The following factors reduce the risk in adopting prototyping tools:

- Conservative technology. It will be easier to gain support and finance if the prototyping tools are unlikely to attract controversy or have already been accepted in the organization. This is especially important if the technical decision may be vetted by other technologists.

- Cultural harmony. Tools may not fit into the organizational culture. For example, they may not come from an accepted supplier or they may require personal computers in a centralized installation. Such tools may be perceived as an excessive risk. This perception is likely to persist no matter how reputable the supplier, how large the benefits, or how excellent the technology.
- Evaluation and late commitment. Unless the tools are employed already in the organization, evaluate them carefully in-house (but within a budget). Avoid irrevocable commitment for as long as possible without delaying genuine progress.
- Use of standards. Use of accepted standards, official or unofficial, should boost confidence in the choice of tools, stabilize change, enhance longevity, and allow greater supplier choice.
- Well-known supplier. A well-known supplier provides a high comfort factor. The supplier probably has earned the reputation, as well, in terms of ability to deliver and support products.

11.2   Cost

Cost is always a major consideration in the adoption of new technology. Adoption cost and the replication cost of target systems is a major component of business effectiveness. These costs may affect the decision to adopt throw-away or evolutionary prototyping strategies. The major factors affecting the costs of adopting prototyping tools are the following:

- Development system. This is the cost of hardware and software needed to run the selected prototyping tools for the expected number of prototype developers. Cost may be affected considerably by the size of the computer chosen to act as the development system or the number of developers.
- Target system. This is the cost of hardware and software needed to run the prototype object in the user environment. If the development and target system are the same, there may be additional costs related to additional users. If the development and target system are not the same, then replication costs will be based on the highly variable cost of the run-time target system.
- Evaluation and adoption. This is the cost associated with selecting a tool, gaining management approval for the tool, obtaining finance, and ordering it. The cost of evaluation and adoption can be surprisingly high, especially if selection is contentious and senior staff become involved. It is not unusual for an evaluation to take a man-year of effort.
- Staffing. It may be felt that present staff are likely to be too resistant to

the uptake of prototyping and its tools. Additional or replacement staff recruitment, temporary or permanent, may be a necessary cost.

- Training. Typical formal training courses for software tools cost £500–1000 per week in the UK. Several weeks training may be required. Fortunately, some tools are sufficiently simple, inherently easy to use, or similar to existing tools that only familiarization is required.
- Familiarization. These are the non-training costs, mainly in loss of productivity, associated with introducing software developers to new tools. Inherent ease of use and similarity with existing tools will affect these costs significantly. Competent staff are likely to finish the process of familiarization after a week, although minor productivity loss may persist for months.

11.3 Functionality of prototyping tools

A prototyping tool is of reduced value if it cannot create the entire prototype within the scope of its own, inherent facilities. This is confirmed by Boar (1984). The following properties assist functionality:

- Complete and convenient provision of operations that are appropriate for solution of the application and for handling irrelevant detail (Smith et al., 1985). Operations commonly required in prototyping typical business applications are logical operations, program flow control, indexed record I/O, record I/O, mathematical operations, character string handling, output formatting, array/record structures, array/record manipulations, and graphical operations.
- Within the context of existing computer operations, there may be functions that are essential to interfacing with other systems. In typical business programming, the most important of these functions is likely to be interface to external databases.
- Ability to escape to different levels of function (e.g. assembler, operating system commands, window servers) is essential if the needed function is not provided within the tool itself.
- Extensibility of the tool (e.g. using functions, subroutines, packages, or objects) is needed to create easily used, robust higher-level functions from lower-level ones.

11.4 Rapid implementation of prototypes

Although rapid development can be over-stressed, as discussed earlier, it is important that modification and testing of prototypes should be as rapid as possible in terms of elapsed time. Rapid prototype development facilitates productive iteration by minimizing the waiting time of those involved in prototyping. Rapid prototyping also helps sustain interest, morale, and motivation in users (Hollinde and Wagner, 1984) and prototypers.

The following software tool features support rapid implementation:

- Readability (Pratt, 1975). This increases the speed of understanding and thus facilitates rapid modification of the prototype (Riddle, 1984).
- Writeability (Pratt, 1975). A terse, compact syntax is quicker to write, even if it may not by easier to read later.
- Interpretation or fast compilation. Interpretation of code eliminates the step of compilation and linking, and thus permits more rapid prototyping than compiled languages. Compilers can employ a number of techniques, such as threaded compilers (Brender, 1978), to speed up their operation.
- Good error-checking and debugging facilities. These greatly help in finding and eliminating errors during prototyping.
- Good run-time performance. This assists rapid evaluation of the prototype by the user and permits some idea of performance to be gained about the final system.
- Modularity. This allows smaller portions of the prototype to be developed and tested, instead of the whole prototype. This speeds development and improves maintainability. Good modularity may also ease some of the problems of interfacing prototypes with existing and future systems. Another aspect of modularity is that it can permit painless substitution of the prototype with target system components (Floyd, 1984).
- 'Power'. Software tools vary in the number of executable statements each source statement invokes (Jones, 1986). The higher this ratio, the more powerful the language. More powerful languages normally facilitate rapid development.
- Extendability. This allows higher-level functions to be assembled and packaged conveniently from lower-level functions. This encourages greater reuse of software and, consequently, faster software development. Some authors consider extendability to be a part of modularity (Riddle, 1984).
- Reusability. Software reused is software that does not have to be written. The quality of reused software is likely to be good, too. Ince (1988) suggests that 40–60 per cent of all software could be reused. Tool features that promote software reuse save both cost and development time.

11.5   Deliverability of prototypes

All prototypes should increase knowledge about their application. A prototype that cannot be delivered easily, however, is likely to prove more expensive than one that can. The following properties promote deliverability:

- Integratability with existing and future systems. The prototype must be capable of efficiently coexisting and interfacing within the total systems of the organization.
- Good run-time performance may enable the prototype to serve as the

delivered system, without modification. The is essential to pursuing an evolutionary prototyping strategy.

- Translatability permits throw-away source prototypes to be converted easily into more efficient object forms. Automatic translation is an exceedingly desirable characteristic.
- Robustness permits the prototype to operate in the presence of accidental and deliberate abuse by users. It may be essential to allow the prototype to serve directly as the target system.
- Testability. It cannot be assumed that even three generations of users will uncover all errors in the prototype. Easy visual checking, computer-assisted structure analysis, and good internal error checking all aid the testing process.
- Scaleability permits prototypes to be converted easily into larger systems or for the prototype itself to be used to handle the live and full-sized application.
- Portability permits the prototype, or its more efficient object form, to be delivered to hosts employing different hardware or operating systems.
- 'Packageability' permits the required prototype function to be presented in a way that is attractive, forgiving, and easy to use (i.e. a good human computer interface). Packageability also permits unwanted tool function to be concealed from the user and the prototype protected from intentional or unintentional abuse by the user.
- Adequate lifetime performance. The performance of the system must remain acceptable throughout the life of the system, even with additional users, greater data volumes, and future functional enhancements.
- Interface to organizational databases. Many organizations employ a common database system. Interface may be essential if the prototype is to be integrated fully with existing and future systems.
- Extensibility or modularity. These permit the incorporation of higher levels of function into the prototype or allow them to be created from the prototype.

11.6 Maintainability of prototypes

Maintenance is the process of both rectifying errors and adding function to the delivered system. Prototyping tools should simplify maintenance, especially if they are to be employed directly as evolutionary prototypes. Maintenance will be important in throwaway prototyping if the prototype is retained as the source for the delivered object program. The following features assist maintainability:

- Readability and compactness assist maintenance. Maintenance ultimately revolves around being able to understand what is being done at the lower level of implementation detail (Kopetz, 1979).

- Constructs that aid good programming style are generally considered beneficial to program maintenance (Dahl *et al.*, 1972).
- Good debugging facilities permit the rapid uncovering of complex and subtle errors in the system. Good debugging features include single-step program execution, variable examination, and change and conditional breakpoints.
- Modularity assists maintenance by permitting the prototype to be rectified or enhanced in smaller, discrete parts that can be integrated easily. Modularity also permits easier understanding of function by permitting unnecessary levels of detail to be abstracted.
- In general, more powerful languages are easier to maintain because the size of the source is smaller. The language selected may affect size by a factor of 20 (Jones, 1986).
- Ideally, the prototyping tool should produce conventional style documentation or produce prototypes directly from conventional documentation (Luqi and Berzins, 1988). At worst, the tool should introduce no major impediments to reverse engineering the system into a more traditional format. An exciting idea, in some environments, is being able to 'back end' fully evaluated prototypes with software engineering tools and techniques.

11.7   Conclusion

Contrary to the views of some authors (e.g. Luqi and Ketabchi, 1988; Tanik and Yeh, 1989), I am far from convinced that special-purpose prototyping tools are essential. Indeed, if the tools selected are too far outside the experience and technology of the developers, they are likely to prove risky and inefficient to adopt. Prototyping does benefit, however, from tools that are complete and precise for expressing the application, yet are natural to the experience and technology of the prototyper.

It is probably safe to say that there are no tools now available that satisfy all the requirements of prototyping. Both conventional and unconventional software tools are available, however, which do permit effective prototyping within most development environments. Therefore, tool selection should not be seen as an impediment to adopting prototyping.

Part Four
Prototyping management and practice

There is no commonly accepted way of practising or managing prototyping. This is not to say, of course, that I have no ideas as to how prototyping should be practised or managed. Some of these ideas are presented in this section. Organizations should take the opportunity, however, of devising their own methods for practice and management of prototyping and for integrating prototyping into their present computing operations. This permits prototyping to be employed in the way that is most culturally and operationally amenable to the organization.

12
Appropriate management styles for prototyping

The need to set time and cost targets and to achieve them is deeply engrained in the current software management culture. The nature of prototyping, being essentially experimental and result oriented, makes it difficult to predict the course and speed of software development by monitoring consumption of resources. It is even more difficult to dictate results with prototyping because users and general management are an integral part of the development process. These aspects of 'unmanageability' challenge the methods and role of many traditional management styles (Mathiassen, 1984).

Management is much concerned with being able to predict and deliver results from the resources available. If excessive emphasis is placed on this aspect, however, there may be adverse side-effects. For one thing, prediction can come to dictate the delivery of results. In other words, results may be moulded to match the prediction, whether the prediction was accurate or not. Meeting the expectations of customers may become a goal of relatively low priority. This seems an almost necessary consequence of measuring management performance by achieving predicted targets, especially if the sole measure is cost or consumption of resources.

One genuinely worried software development manager, an engineer, said to me recently, 'If we use prototyping, how will I know whether I'm going to hit my targets or not?' He was not greatly reassured by my reply that he could walk down to the users and actually watch the software working to see if his targets were being hit. To him, the notion of managing software development by monitoring the results achieved, rather than resources consumed, seemed totally alien. Of course, only prototyping makes this possible because interim results are produced during software development.

12.1 The need for management change

A major shift in management style and thinking is required to create a climate for the most effective prototyping. This shift can be one of the most difficult steps to take. An appropriate computing management style for prototyping should take into account the following factors:

- The in-built motivation of most computing technologists.
- The improbability of full and accurate analysis before software development.
- The difficulty of accurate time estimation (W. Myers, 1989).
- The need for flexibility throughout development.

12.2 Predicting development time and cost

Most computing managers, even those operating purely internal services, operate under strong pressure from their higher management to predict the time and cost of software development accurately and to meet their predictions. I call this 'time-driven management'. If software managers wish to keep their jobs, then they must ensure, one way or another, that their operations meet their predictions. Meeting time and cost targets is likely to become much more important than giving users satisfaction or competitive edge to the organization.

It is worth understanding why higher management wants time and cost predictions for software development. The obvious, and legitimate, reasons are as follows:

- Establishing costs before development to allow budgeting.
- Allocating resources and controlling their use.
- Setting long-term schedules with other parts of the organization.
- Preparing the organization for delivery of the software.

A less worthy reason for 'prediction-driven management' may be that higher management simply does not trust its computing management with the resources given to it. Higher management are also likely not to be sufficiently competent to judge the quality and efficiency of its software management. Consequently, prediction, especially time predictions, end up being used as 'whips' for software management, rather than fulfilling legitimate business goals. This type of tight control appears to be characteristic of computer operations undergoing a 'mid-life crisis' (Nolan, 1979).

Prediction of time is one of the weakest parts of the software development process, whether traditional, software engineering, or prototyping approaches are adopted. The fatal flaw of all prediction schemes is that accurate analysis of the problem is needed in advance. Accurate analysis, in advance of solution, as I have tried to show already, is exceedingly difficult. Formal methods to predict software development times are complex, labour intensive, and time consuming (Boehm, 1981). The estimating tools are expensive and there is no standard method. I suspect that the cost of using formal prediction methods could in some cases rival the cost of developing the software itself. Formal estimation methods are not particularly relevant in the small to medium-size computing department because of their cost, complexity, and manpower requirements.

It must be remembered, too, that software development predictions do not exist solely within the technical environment. The estimates that a software manager makes may be reasonable (Metzger, 1981) from a purely technical point of view. These predictions, however, are generally subject to external influences of varying strengths, e.g. demands from higher management to cut costs, insistence by customers for early delivery, or events such as the end of the budgeting year. Computer managers almost inevitably are forced to change some or all of their predictions to satisfy these pressures. Typically, they will be under pressure to deliver more function, in less time, and at a lower cost than they believe is possible. Unfortunately, a software development conceived at Christmas may simple not be ready to deliver before the end of the tax year on 1 April. Efforts to hasten the event may result in failure of the project.

One of the most obvious fallacies of time-driven management is that computing managers are asked to prepare the very time-scales that will later be used to judge their performance. Curiously, questions rarely seem to be asked about how the time predictions are obtained. Most software managers soon learn to apply coarse rules of thumb to software estimation, such as 'ten lines of tested program per day' or 'a day's work for each database field'. These rules work mainly because they lead to gross overestimation of the amount of time required and, therefore, provide a comfortable safety margin for the development process. If software managers know they will be expected to revise their estimates downward, they may respond with even greater overestimates. Correspondingly, higher management may learn to respond with demands for even more savage cuts. Estimates can spiral out of control.

Some organizations accept estimates without negotiation. Quite rightly, they may say that the tendency to overestimate is just as bad as to underestimate. Here, the software manager with a stronger sense of survival than honour simply continues to overestimate and then under-works to meet the schedule. Honourable, and possibly naîve, software managers shorten their estimates until they can no longer meet their targets. Then they are in trouble. The result, in either case, is almost always friction, slow delivery of software, or waste.

Predicting time and cost in prototyping may be even more difficult because of the uncertain number of iterations that may be required. Lack of experience in estimating for prototypes also may be a worry (Mayhew et al., 1989). Predicting costs in prototyping, especially costs unrelated to labour, such as hardware costs, may be particularly difficult if the evolutionary approach is taken. Here, it may prove necessary to overcome performance deficiencies through the unanticipated purchase of more powerful hardware or by having to translate the prototype into a more efficient form.

The general inability of software managers to predict software development time and the lack of acceptable formal methods for prediction leads to an almost inescapable conclusion, namely that it is un-realistic to expect to be able to predict software development accurately, cost-effectively, and repeatably. Management based on the presupposition of accurate time estimation, therefore, is fatally flawed. Failure to meet time promises may be a major contributor to the perception of failure in computing operations. This is because software developers, time and time again, find that they cannot meet the promises they have made.

12.3   Problems of time-driven management

One of the most important traditional management functions is that of prediction. I have attempted to show that the predictability of software is generally dubious or too expensive for internal computing operations. The absurdity of trying to drive custom software development by time can be seen in our hypothetical gourmet restaurant. Imagine the reaction to a customer who rushes in off the street and says, 'I want dinner. I want it in 15 minutes, on the dot! Oh, yes, it had better be good, too!' In a high-quality restaurant, the manager would probably have the wisdom and integrity to suggest that the diner cuts along to the nearest hamburger stand for a couple of cheeseburgers. An unscrupulous restaurant will take last week's leftovers from the deep freeze, pop them into the microwave for 5 minutes and then wait 10 minutes to serve them. A foolish restaurant will genuinely try to meet the customer's demand; moreover, it will almost certainly fail to satisfy him.

Another problem of time-driven management is that it presupposes that the development of software is a mechanical process. It is assumed that the relationship between time and output is a simple one: time equals output. This denies the reality of software development and the possibility of a creative element in it. The reality is that sometimes development goes very quickly and sometimes it goes very slowly; it rarely appears to move at a steady pace. The slowing effect seems especially noticeable towards the end of a project. This particularly is the time at which it is exceedingly unwise to add more manpower (Metzger, 1981).

Unfortunately, software development managers fall for time-driven management pressure, over and over again. Time-driven management usually is neither beneficial nor necessary for software development, especially in internal computing operations. Inaccurate prediction of development time contributes to a number of problems:

- Over or under cost run.
- Deterioration of quality or function.
- Loss of confidence in the computing operation.
- Operational difficulty and inefficiency (e.g. users waiting for delivery, capital equipment idle).

To meet the demands of imposed time schedules, computing management may respond with strategems that encourage waste and greatly increase the risk of unsuccessful implementation. The following responses are typical:

- Premature delivery of software. Here, the software is handed over to the users on the appointed delivery date, irrespective of whatever state it is in at that time. Computing management then declares that their software has been delivered 'on time' and shifts development into the maintenance phase. Users are saddled with unfinished, untested, undocumented, or error-prone software.
- Reduction of software function. In this strategem, software management detects in advance that the software will be late. Functions, possibly vital ones, are eliminated from the delivery, often without consultation. Users are given subfunctional software which may or may not be finished during maintenance.
- Increased manpower. Additional staff are applied to the late development, either from other projects or by hiring outside staff. Not only does this strategem usually 'rob Peter to pay Paul', but staff introduced late into any project are more likely to slow delivery than to accelerate it (Metzger, 1981).

The pity of this situation is that a time-driven style of management is usually not necessary for internal computing operations because their costs and staffing are fixed. Development forced into maintenance will not save money, since the same people will be doing the work and at the same cost to the business. Nor are programming staff likely to be greatly influenced by establishing arbitrary time targets. They may, if harassed sufficiently by demands to produce on time, work less efficiently and disrupt more users. Time targets mainly establish that software management cannot accurately predict the time required for software development. This fact hardly requires much additional verification.

12.4 Management by priority

Rather than being obsessed with the time of software delivery, a more effective means of providing a management framework for prototyping may be to:

- Establish the software functions the organization needs.
- Prioritize these needs.
- Work to deliver the functions in sequence of priority.

I call this management by priority. Management by priority requires a determined effort to:

- Determine the range of applications that are needed within the organization.
- Agree and establish the priority in which the applications are needed.
- Establish the validity and range of any time constraints for the applications.
- Define the necessary degree of user and business satisfaction (i.e. quality) required for each application.
- Establish the resources available to develop the applications.

In management by priority, internal software development management does not give timed delivery commitments; higher management does not demand them. Performance in management by priority is measured by producing adequate quality applications, in the desired sequence, within the available resources. Where applications genuinely must be completed with a time frame, then these should be given highest priority and completed as quickly as possible. Better still, this software should if possible be purchased from somewhere else.

Prototyping greatly supports management by priority because this approach gives management a continuous and easily understood means of assessing the real progress and quality of its software development. Correspondingly, management by priority is compatible with prototyping because artificial time pressures are de-emphasized in favour of satisfying the need to have applications completed to a desired quality.

Time-driving managers will probably consider management by priority naïve. They will say 'People won't work without deadlines' or ask 'How will we know where we are in the project if we don't have deadlines?' The general lack of success of software applications and time estimation (W. Myers, 1989) should be well known. Any faith in time estimates for software development is exceedingly naïve. Any organization that depends seriously on the timing of internal software development is taking an unacceptable business risk. The only way of ensuring on-time delivery is to have the software developed or acquired before it is required. Timed installation, therefore, can only be safely committed when the necessary software is completely finished and tested.

Another departure from the time-driven management style is that the management by priority style presupposes that computing management can be trusted to run a reasonably efficient operation. In my experience, most computing organizations are reasonably efficient, within the constraints of their culture, history, and resouces. Typically, no one in higher management is sufficiently competent to judge the technical efficiency of computing operations. Computing management efficiency should be judged on long-term results of delivering software that genuinely meets user and business needs. It should not be judged on meeting arbitrary time schedules drawn up under pressure to predict what is essentially unpredictable.

12.5 Leadership and prototyping

Leadership is an important human quality that is given only lip-service by many organizations. The concept, as leadership, is particularly neglected in computing. Leadership, however, may be the most effective management technique for achieving constant and reproducible success in software development, especially in prototyping. There is no easy formula for achieving leadership. Some of the demands of leadership may seem alien to the introverted nature of many computer technologists (Weinberg, 1971). All the traits of leadership are valuable to anyone engaged in prototyping.

The following are some general leadership traits and techniques (Stackpole, 1962):

- Knowledge of the subject and of the technology involved. People respond well to a manager who genuinely knows what needs to be done and how to do it. Do not attempt to be omniscient; instead, be generally knowledgeable and know where to seek in-depth knowledge when necessary. Keep yourself informed about business as well as technical matters.
- Be decisive and resolute. Managers, no matter how good their knowledge, cannot lead if they are unable to make justifiable decisions promptly. Few decisions in software development are ever completely wrong or completely right. A less-than-optimum decision, if rapidly, reasonably, and resolutely carried out, is usually preferable to an optimum decision endlessly prolonged.
- Keep people informed. Take every opportunity, and make opportunities, to keep everyone who has anything to do with your operation informed. Let them know what you expect to do, tell them how you are going to do it, and say why you are doing what you do. Do not be afraid of being a bit of a bore, as long as you do not bore with technology. Informing people is so important that it is good practice to keep a list of people you should contact. Make sure that you do so on a regular basis.
- See and be seen. Make sure that anyone can see you at the shortest possible notice. Make sure that you get out of your office and see what is going on. A daily stroll around your staff and users will pay off handsomely in information and presence. Look over people's shoulders, see what they are doing, and talk to them about what they are doing. You may be surprised what you find out.

- Overcome problems and make sure people know it. The maxim 'nothing succeeds like success' is only too true. Real challenges are exciting, but ensure that you win most of the time. Make sure, in a modest way, that people know that you are winning.
- Get your hands dirty some of the time. Programming managers, no matter how much experience they have had in the past, will have a hard time maintaining the respect of their programmers and their own grip on reality if they do not do some software development from time to time. Do not do just the interesting parts, but tasks such as data entry, documentation, and operating as well. Make sure, however, that your participation is planned and does not interfere with your primary role.

Probably the most important aspect of leadership is respect. Software managers must respect themselves, their users, their staff, and their management. This respect must be reciprocated. It is difficult to develop software successfully where any group or major personality involved in a development scorns another. Software managers are unfortunate that their positions often do not inherently command the respect, status, and authority accorded to most management positions. Because of this, they must work tirelessly to achieve and maintain the respect of their staff, users, and management.

12.6 Conclusion

Management often contributes to both real and perceived software failure by insisting, sometimes quite unnecessarily, on arbitrary deadlines for the completion of software. This either results in failure to deliver the software on time or in the use of strategems by software management, at the expense of efficiency, to ensure that software is delivered on time. In the internal software operations of small and medium-sized organizations, there is usually no need to deliver software to a particular schedule. Waste is difficult for the smaller business to support. If software is genuinely needed for a particular time, then it is best to purchase it off the shelf, rather than to attempt to develop it.

The usual reason for setting time goals is as a means for non-technical management to measure the supposed progress of software development and, thereby, assure themselves that all is well. They also hope to constrain labour-related costs. Historically, however, accurate prediction of the time it will take to produce custom software has proven almost universally inaccurate, and there is no sign that this situation will improve. Organizations that depend on the timed delivery of custom software are putting themselves at serious risk. Given that time-based management does not 'work' for managing software, it is only sensible to seek a different approach.

What management really should be seeking, in most cases, is the fastest possible delivery of adequate software with the least waste and friction. Properly led and managed, this is what prototyping can deliver. Management at all levels can and should involve itself in prototyping. By doing so, they can contribute to the software itself. At the same time, they can assure themselves that efficient progress is being made. This, however, takes a considerable shift in the present attitude of both software and general management. There is no pat formula for causing this to happen. This is a change that only management itself can make.

13
Management issues in prototyping

One of the main worries about adopting prototyping is managing it (Ince, 1989). This worry is far from trivial since prototyping may offer a quick path to software anarchy if it is not properly managed. It is important, therefore, that both general management and computing management understand the steps required in the practice of prototyping and ensure that the necessary controls are maintained.

Some of the management issues likely to be perceived about prototyping are the following:

- The role of the software manager.
- The role of the prototyping manager.
- Friction between users and prototypers.
- Public exposure of interim success and failure.
- Knowing when to stop and when to keep going.
- Maintaining business relevance and validity.
- Maintaining technical quality and standards.
- Defining deliverables.
- Monitoring and evaluating success.

13.1 The role of the software manager

In all but the smallest computing operations, there is likely to be a level of management that is responsible for prototyping, but does not actually control it. This is the software manager—a role that can be critical to the success of the prototyping effort. The role of the software manager is concerned with political and organizational issues. Software managers must appreciate the political aspects of their role as too many software developments fail in this area. There is little point in achieving a technical success within a political failure.

A part of achieving political success in most organizations is to provide a convincing appearance of management. Software managers should always remember the saying, 'If you want to live with wolves, howl like a wolf.' Some useful means for software managers to 'howl' like a manager are as follows:

- Careful tracking of resources for which you are responsible. Give short, regular, and quantitative reports to your management on resource utilization, particularly that of staff and costs. This shows that you are 'business-minded' and careful in your use of resources. Use project management software to plan, document, and track progress. Ensure that this is employed in communication to higher management.

- If you are not being asked to produce regular management reports, then you are either not being taken seriously, work for a badly run organization, or produce such boring and irrelevant monthly reports that nobody wants to read them. The regular report is your opportunity to tell everyone how well everything is going (in one or two sentences), how busy you are, warn them gently of upcoming problems, and to let them know how much money you are saving or making for them. Submit the report on time and keep it short. Do not discuss technical problems unless specifically asked to do so; if you must, keep technical discussions very short.

- Computing staff tend to have an unfortunate tendency to despise all administration as mindless bureaucracy. Administration may or may not serve a useful function in the organization, but it unquestionably does exist. Moreover, administration usually has considerable power and influence in the host organization; it can make a lot of trouble. Since computing people are always suspected of being anarchists, closet or otherwise, it is wise to take the approach of being scrupulous about satisfying administrative functions. Administration is not nearly as onerous as it looks, especially if one is organized to do it intelligently.

- Ensure, through education and discussion, that expectations and goals of higher management are realistic in the first place. This saves a lot of trouble, in the long run, and fosters good relations: education is a good way to soften antagonists.

Software managers should not do these things cynically. If they cannot see that these activities are genuinely useful, then they should seriously consider if software management is really a career they should be pursuing. If they fail to undertake these activities, then they will contribute seriously to the possibility of failure of all aspects of their operation.

13.2 The role of the prototyping manager

Prototyping managers are responsible for the day-to-day operation of prototype developments. They may also be the sole prototypers of the operation, they may control a number of prototypers, or they may do no prototyping themselves. These managers must be the 'architects' (Mason and Carey, 1983) of the prototype. The technical responsibilities of these managers in a prototyping development might include the following:

• Establishing designs and interfaces.
• Decomposing the application, if necessary.
• Responsibility for integration and testing.
• Achieving organizational objectives.
• Containing and moulding management and user expectations.

It is a particularly serious mistake, though it may be a tempting one, for prototyping managers to leave design of the prototype to the users or to prototypers working 'on the front line'. Many design decisions must be taken in a much wider context than that of the immediate development. Technical management has the sole responsibility to ensure that the context of their development is appropriate to the computing infrastructure. Experienced designers may also be able to contribute a clearer insight into the structure of the application than users (Jorgensen, 1984).

Prototyping managers should concentrate strongly on control of the resources involved in the development. The main resource to be controlled by management is the staff involved in the prototype development. Computing staff need management support to do the following:

• Help maintain focus on the problem.
• Ensure contact with users.
• Finish the last part of the development.
• Re-establish their confidence when things go badly.
• Restrain their 'gold plating' and 'creeping excellence' tendencies.

Computing staff are not the only ones involved in prototyping, of course. A good prototyping manager will certainly not neglect the problems and needs of the users and managers involved in or affected by the prototype.

13.3 Friction between users and prototypers

It is almost inevitable that conflict will arise between users and prototypers at some point during the development of the prototype. One would naturally expect considerable conflict during the early stages of prototyping, but the period towards the end of a project can also be an especially dangerous time. By then, most of the team will have become fatigued with the development. Undesirable friction can arise easily at this point and will be more difficult to dissipate than earlier in the project.

Surprisingly, a certain amount of conflict is useful, particuarly at the early stages of development. Conflict can serve to expose issues that otherwise might not arise. Total lack of conflict or unusually passive users should be a warning to developers that these users are not participating in the prototype. Too much or uncontrolled conflict, on the other hand, can reach the ears of those outside the project, create an undesirable image, or cause permanent interpersonal damage. A good way of preventing this might be to have regular 'conflict sessions' away from the office and to forbid open conflict in the work place.

It is good prototyping management practice, therefore, not to suppress all forms of conflict between the users and developers. Good management will channel and use this conflict constructively. Managers must ensure, however, that conflict is resolved before it damages the project or 'spills out' of the project and hurts its reputation. Where users and development staff have purely personal conflicts, managers should either attempt to resolve these quickly or to relocate the problem people with as little disruption as possible. Managers also should watch out for signs of staff fatigue and be prepared to rotate people, when necessary, to relieve it.

13.4 Public exposure of success and failure

Prototyping necessarily involves a great deal of exposure of the software at all stages of development. The positive side of this is that users are exposed to the frequent coups and excitement that software development brings. If general management or a wider audience (Livesey, 1984) are involved in the prototyping process, then there is an opportunity for the computing operation to show that it can produce good results rapidly and without the traditional friction between developers and users.

The negative side of prototyping, of course, is that many of the failures will be open to public criticism. There is nothing more irritating to a prototyper than to have a flaw exposed in front of everyone. The cry of 'See, I told you, the system is no good!' may be taken up for even the most trivial problem. Prototypers not only must attempt to hold their tongues at this point, but must also try to understand why the users are reacting in this way. Often, this is a symptom of anxiety in the users, who may be genuinely unaware that the flaw is trivial.

Computer managers can reduce the problems of public failure in several ways:

- Careful and unsympathetic testing before demonstration to eliminate the possibility of crashes and outright technical errors. Silly and careless mistakes will undermine user confidence.
- Intelligent and low-key defence of honest errors of interpretation, but ready acceptance of the need to correct them. Prototypers need a certain

degree of humility, but need not become 'doormats' for user hostility. Mutual respect is the best relationship for prototyping.

• A well-known 'track record' of successful past software implementation. This builds and sustains confidence and respect. This implies the need for a certain talent at self-advertisement.

Some public failure should not necessarily be considered a bad thing. In limited doses, failure may help users to realize that programmers are as human as everyone else. It may also be valuable in trimming back some of the prototypers' natural arrogance. It also shows users that prototypers are listening and responding to what they are saying. One valuable aspect of public failure made good is to show users that programming is not easy, but that problems can be overcome.

13.5   Knowing when to stop and when to keep going

One of the concerns often expressed about prototyping is deciding when to stop working on the prototype. Surprisingly, I have rarely found this to be a problem, and Mayhew *et al.* (1989) confirm this finding. Two or three iterations should be adequate if the users are really telling the prototyper what they want and if the prototyper really is listening. One cannot afford to be doctrinaire about the number of iterations permitted, however, otherwise much of the benefit will be lost.

The ideal point at which to stop is when the benefits being produced are costing more to produce than they are worth. The problem is, of course, deciding what is the cost and value. There is no pat formula. Basically, it is up to management to decide, for better or for worse, when prototyping must stop. There should be no reason prototyping cannot be resumed later, if necessary. Finishing prototyping is a bit like visiting someone; it is usually better to leave too soon than it is to leave too late.

Tingley (1984) poses an interesting problem. If a prototype works well, then user job security may be threatened seriously. Users will be well positioned to see this threat and could be able to sabotage or delay the development by proposing extreme cases. I have seen this reaction, but have found that it usually occurs at the early stages of prototyping. This problem is one in which both computer and general management should be asked to intervene. If the prototype is adequate, then the software manager must verify this and be prepared to bring the problem to the attention of general management. General management will either have to decide in favour of job security or business efficiency.

In my experience, stopping is not usually a serious problem in prototyping. More often the problem is to keep on going right to the end of the project. Users and prototypers tend to get tired long before the prototype is completed; tempers can become frayed; users start falling behind their 'real' work. For users, fatigue is usually not as serious a problem as it is for developers. When the users get tired, it is usually a sign that prototyping can stop. Developers ususally become fatigued when the rapid gratification and excitement of development slows. This is sometimes known as the '90 per cent finished syndrome'. Documentation is a particularly tiresome hurdle for most software developers and it often comes at this point.

The ideal for the prototyping manager would be to have a team of traditional software developers who would love to do nothing but 'clean up other people's messes', i.e. finish the work of the prototypers. Unfortunately, there are not many software developers who like to maintain or clean up other people's work. Software managers must keep at their prototypers to finish the project completely. Encourage them, incentivize them, rotate them, threaten them, beg them, or do it yourself: just make sure the job is finished properly. It is as simple as that.

13.6 Maintaining business relevance and validity

Prototyping must satisfy the business as well as users. Occasional 'sanity checks' (Metzger, 1981) are needed. There is a danger that successful prototyping could help individual users promulgate serious business fallacies and myopic viewpoints unless some form of business control and validation is exercised. This problem is hardly unique to prototyping, of course, except that users are more likely to get what they actually demand with prototyping.

A business review board (BRB, see Fig. 13.1) is one means of exerting guidance in this area of concern and ensuring top level contribution to software development. The ideal board would be composed of topmost management or senior representatives from within the organization. The software manager should be a member of the BRB.

The BRB might prepare guidelines for each prototype development. These guidelines might outline the following:

- Scope of the prototype.
- Maximum allowable costs.
- Maximum time to be allocated to the prototype.
- Users to be involved in the prototype.
- Areas of the organization likely to be affected.
- Outline business techniques to be employed.
- Termination criteria.

A BRB should be concerned primarily with defining business-critical objectives, data, and function. Prototypes would probably be the most effective means of allowing the board to validate that software development was best supporting the objectives of the organization. In some organizations, a BRB might also be employed to help manage the overall prototyping effort

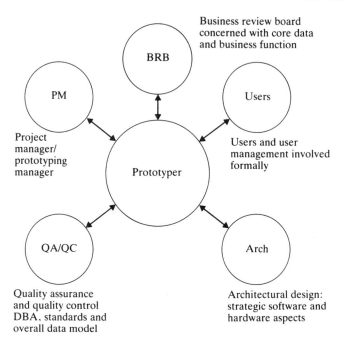

Figure 13.1   A general management structure for prototyping

in terms of deciding on development priorities and objectives. This is especially valuable as a means of effecting more appropriate styles of management.

13.7   Maintaining technical quality and standards

The internal technical quality of prototypes is a serious issue. Deterioration of internal quality and standards can adversely affect costs, long-term maintenance, and efficiency. Probably the most vital area in which technical standards must be applied is in the database. Control in this area, fortunately can be imposed by the database administrator.

The quality and style of implementation, documentation, and user interfaces are matters of much more than local concern. Some degree of global quality control should be exercised in these areas, especially in larger computer operations.

Larger organizations will probably have formal technical quality assurance/ quality control (QA/QC) and database standards functions established. These technical functions can advise prototypers and prototyping managers on a detailed level about expected standards and quality assurance procedures. In a typical database management system based (see Chap. 15) prototype, QA/QC control might be exercised on only areas that directly affect users or other parts of the system (Fig. 13.2). Organizations without QA/QC functions should take steps to ensure that prototypers are conversant with and responsible for adhering to expected quality and standards.

Every prototype should probably commence with at least a simple statement about the expected quality of the final product. This statement has, in particular, implications for the termination criteria. It is easy for quality and standards functions to get out of control, though, and start to control the whole process. It must be remembered that maximum quality is not necessarily an efficient goal, especially in some forms of prototyping. Prototyping managers should ensure that the quality and standards functions are supporting prototypers, not hindering them unnecessarily.

13.8 Deliverables

The main deliverable of prototyping is the prototype itself. This may sound obvious, but software management sometimes appears to lose sight of the real goal of their operation: to produce working software. Within the activities described above, a number of more detailed deliverables can be proposed. The following check-list was devised to indicate some possible deliverables and responsibilities arising from a prototype (Table 13.1).

Many organizations depend on data models of various types (Webster, 1988) to describe overall data structure. Prototypes themselves typically do nothing directly to describe data structure. Manipulations of the data structure are often embedded fairly cryptically within the prototype itself. Addi-

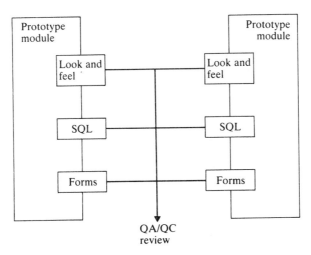

Figure 13.2 Quality control and prototyping

Table 13.1 Prototype deliverables and responsibilities

Deliverable	User	Prototyper	Prototyping Manager	QC/OA	BRB
Data model of the prototype	no	no	some	yes	no
Describe technical function	no	yes	some	some	no
Describe business function	some	some	yes	no	some
Unresolved issues	some	some	some	some	yes
Demonstration and education	some	yes	some	some	some
Next phase information	some	some	yes	some	some
Next phase commitment	no	no	some	no	yes

tional work may be needed to document the data structure and the relationship of the prototype to it. Asking the prototypers to do this task may be an inefficient use of their time. I suggest that the quality control manager should be responsible for producing data models with the assistance of the prototyping manager.

The internal technical functions, operations, and algorithms of the prototype may not be evident from viewing the prototype or even its source program. The prototyper should be responsible for documenting these functions, either within the source or separately. The prototyping manager should act as the collecting agent and reviewer of these functions. In an environment in which the quality is tightly controlled, this documentation might be subjected to formal review.

Just as internal operation may not be immediately evident, the business function of the prototype may not be transparent to others. Users should contribute to this description with the prototyping manager acting as the responsible agent. The business review board should review this description and place it within the greater context of the organization.

It may be impossible to resolve all the necessary issues that arise during development of a prototype. Prototyping may also uncover unexpected issues. It is important that these are collected by the prototyping manager during development and communicated to the appropriate functions. Final dispatch of unresolved issues should be the remit of the business review board.

Much of the value of prototyping is lost if the results are not demonstrated and the organization is not educated by the prototype. Before prototyping starts, the business review board should indicate the areas of the organization that should be affected by the prototype. They might also point out areas that should be educated. Through the prototyping manager, it is the responsibility of the prototyper to carry out this programme of demonstration and education. If this aspect is to be emphasized, it might be advisable to establish a separate function for this purpose.

An individual prototype may not be the end of development. Organizations may wish to redevelop using traditional approaches or to instigate another phase of prototyping. The development of a prototype may point towards the need for other developments. The following are some of the points to detail for the next phase:

- Degree of likely modularization.
- Possible development approaches (e.g. package, analysis).
- Internal or external development suitability.
- Priority recommendations.
- Time and cost expectations.
- Tool and architectural issues.
- Quality level recommendations.

All those involved in the prototype may have information that is germane to the next phase. Commitment to move to the next phase should be made by the business review board with the agreement of the prototyping manager. This might be the point at which the board issues its guidelines for the next phase.

13.9 Evaluating prototyping success

The difficulty of quantifying success was presented in Part One. Any reasonable scheme of regular, quantitative measurement is probably better than none at all, even if it is only really useful for providing a conventional appearance of management. For example, when dealing with your own management, you are more likely to present a credible front when asked how prototyping is working if you can reply, 'Producing 45.7 lines of code per day, up 14.7 per cent over the same time last year' instead of 'Ummm, we're probably doing OK.' Quantitative measurements will probably help you to evaluate the effectiveness of your operation. Problems are likely to start, however, if you take these figures too seriously. A 14.7 per cent rise in 'productivity' may not be significant. On the other hand, a rise of 150 per cent is likely to mean something. Measurements that may prove convincing are lines of source program, number of errors reported, or changes requested.

Opinion polls and surveys are used extensively in other walks of life. Sensibly conducted, these can provide some convincing measures of success or failure in prototyping, even though your surveys might be disputed academically. Imagine the impact of being able to claim, with justification, that 'User satisfaction has improved 50 per cent since prototyping was introduced.' Before adopting prototyping, conduct simple regular, possibly monthly, opinion polls of your users and their management. The audience should be representative and one that your users and management will respect. Some of the questions asked might be:

- Do you feel that our computing services give good value to you?
- Are you confident that our computing staff are technically competent?
- Do you feel that our computing staff understand your business problems and are sympathetic towards them?
- Do you find our computing staff friendly, helpful, and easy to approach?
- Do you think our computing services respond fast enough to meet your business needs?
- How would you rate your level of useful knowledge and insight about how computers can be used in your business?
- Do you think we are ahead of or behind our competitors in the effectiveness of our computing services?
- Do you think we are ahead of our customers or behind them in the effectiveness of our computing services?

If the same group of people are surveyed regularly during the transition to prototyping, major shifts in attitude should provide a strong indication of the success or failure of prototyping, at least from the user perspective, in your organization. Naturally, part of the group should not be affected by prototyping so that it can act as a control.

13.10   Conclusion

The issues confronting management over prototyping are not particularly special to prototyping. The solutions to the prototyping management issues are largely a matter of experience, planning, imagination, and common sense. Flexible attitudes and genuine ability are the most valuable management resource for extracting maximum benefit from prototyping. The lack of an established tradition for prototyping should not be seen as an impediment to its adoption, but rather as an opportunity to devise a practice that exactly matches the needs of the host organization.

14
Structure of prototyping

Most managers have come to expect to see explicit structures for all software development approaches. Although there is no established life cycle for prototyping, a general framework for prototyping can be proposed (Fig. 14.1). Each of the activities within this general framework require more detailed discussion.

14.1 Planning

I recommend that all prototypes should have a written business context to establish the need and expectations for the system being prototyped. This should include simple statements of the following:

- Business function of the target system.
- Expected costs.

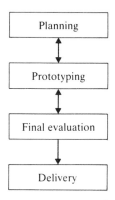

Figure 14.1 A general prototyping framework

- Expected benefits.
- Expected life of the target system.
- Relationship to other systems and business functions.
- Agreed constraints.

An excellent way of establishing a need for a prototype at an appropriate level is to conduct a rigorous and business-oriented cost–benefit analysis such as that suggested by King and Schrems (1978). This type of analysis establishes the need for a proposed system in terms of tangible, monetary returns from reduced or avoided costs and better utilization of assets and capital.

Before commencing implementation, the user, the prototyper, software management, and general management should plan the prototype with care. Even traditional analysis and specification approaches can be valuable at this stage. Analysis should not become so protracted as to destroy the *élan* of prototyping (i.e. no 'analysis to paralysis'). The prototype specification should briefly clarify the following in writing:

- The prototyping strategy (throw-away or evolutionary) to be employed.
- The scope (full or partial, breadboard or mock-up) of the prototype; if partial, define which parts will be prototyped.
- Target system users, their interface requirements, and training needs.
- Target system hardware and software.
- Earliest and latest useful delivery dates for the prototype.
- Interface to external systems, functions, and data.
- Performance needs and criteria.
- Target system maintenance needs and procedures.
- People involved and their specific responsibility, authority, and time commitment.
- Prototype and target system acceptance criteria and arbitration procedures.
- The functions of the prototype in as much detail as needed to commence implementation.
- Any historical analysis and development documentation that might be available.
- All existing manual and computer forms and reports associated with the application.

Although it may sound blindingly obvious to say so, I would advise prototypers to plan to do the easiest and most needed functions first. Most of the measurable economic benefits of computing come from fairly simple, routine applications (King, 1983) and it is easiest to get users' attention for something that they need urgently. There are also considerable psychological advantages in being seen to have successes as early as possible in the development.

Interface definition and design for prototypes should be an essential part of planning in large projects (Boehm, 1987) or where the final system must coexist with other systems. Here, Boehm *et al.*, (1984, p. 299) suggest that prototypes 'should be followed by a reasonable level of specification. . .and. . .interfaces'. Few systems exist outside of the context of other systems and the general trend in computing seems to be towards greater integration and standardization. It would be exceedingly unwise to assume any significant degree of independence of any system. Consequently careful planning for integration of the prototype is needed.

14.2   Contracts and charging

In some environments, a formal contract should be considered (IT-STARTS, 1989a; Mayhew *et al.*, 1989; Metzger, 1981) in addition to a prototype specification. The following are some of the additional aspects that might be considered:

- Price or charging arrangements (e.g. time and materials, fixed price, royalties).
- Mechanisms for dealing with issues outside of the original specification of the work.
- Mechanisms, criteria, and procedures for reporting, control, completion, and acceptance.

Charging is a difficult issue in prototyping. If external agencies are employed for prototyping, then this may be an important business issue. If the computing service is internal to the host organization, charging is largely an irrelevant issue. Not making an internal profit, however, can become a serious political problem in some organizations.

In general prototyping is not well suited to firm, fixed-price contracts (Metzger, 1981). The fixed-delivery specifications required are alien to the prototyping approach. Variations on the time and materials theme are well suited from the prototyper's viewpoint. This may not suit the host organization, however. A fixed expenditure ceiling for time and materials seems a realistic control, since every organization should know how much it is prepared to spend on any software development. Human nature being what it is, though, it must be expected that development costs will inevitably reach that ceiling. The ceiling effectively then becomes just another fixed-price contract.

An effective strategy for prototype charging may be to negotiate a series of fixed-price contracts as development proceeds. Initially, the value of the contracts would be small, but would presumably grow as development proceeds. The need to recontract helps control costs and provides a strong incentive for the prototyper to perform satisfactorily. This arrangement has the disadvantage of requiring frequent renegotiation and creating insecurity for the developer. A charging strategy that does not have these disadvantages, yet limits costs effectively, may be to use rolling contracts for time and materials. Here, the contract is automatically renewed every day unless explicitly cancelled. This ensures that the host organization is never committed for more than the period of the contract and the developer has a relative degree of security.

One thing to remember is that there are no bargains in software development. The best strategy for charging is to decide to pay a fair price for good work. How this is done is mainly a matter of format. This advice may sound idealistic, but it is not. It is simply a matter of pure self-interest.

14.3 Prototyping

Turning needs and plans into a target system requires implementation of a prototype. Boar (1984) characterizes the nature of the early part of prototype implementation as concentrating on the following:

- Gaining broad acceptance of the proposed solution.
- Detection of major oversights.
- Achieving user familiarity and 'comfort'.

The later parts of development tend to shift towards:

- Adding function.
- Correcting function.
- Evaluating ideas and suggestions from the user.
- Improving the user interface.

Successful prototype implementation requires:

- Prototypers with considerable patience and tact.
- Prototypers with excellent skill in programming.
- Users who place a high priority on evaluating the prototype when it is ready.
- Users with expert knowledge, some patience, and a critical turn of mind.
- Users with a genuine interest in the software product being developed.
- Management with reasonable expectations and realistic time-scales.

In my experience, the most effective prototyping involves two types of people: highly competent prototypers and knowledgeable, interested end-users. Once implementation has commenced, the prototypers will usually work alone much of the time to produce major parts of the prototype. During this time they will probably require frequent access to the users to ask questions. When ready, the prototypers will demonstrate their work to the users who will comment on its suitability. Preferably, the users will themselves try the software. If possible, the prototypers will make corrections immediately and evaluate these corrections with the users beside them. The prototypers will then return for another round of development and the cycle will continue until the users are satisfied.

Earlier, I commented that some authors (e.g. Tanik and Yeh, 1989) might be emphasizing excessively the speed that prototyping can bring to the development process. While rapid development is not the most significant distinction of prototyping, it is important to prototype quickly enough to sustain the attention of the users and to maintain intellectual momentum. Riddle (1984) suggests that if the prototype cannot be 'brought up' within three days, then the scope of the problem should be reduced. I think there is considerable wisdom in this approach, although it would not be wise to be doctrinaire about it.

While users need not be dedicated full time to the implementation, it is important that they are reasonably available whenever the prototyper needs them. It is possible, of course, for one user to work with several prototypers concurrently, and vice versa. Users who have been involved in prototypes before are generally a great deal more help to prototypers than inexperienced ones.

It may be necessary and wise to employ several users of different expertise on complex problems. If the software product is to be employed by anyone other than the user, as usually is the case, then it is essential that the evaluation process be repeated with at least one other user to eliminate any idiosyncrasies of the first user. As a rule, prototype evaluation by three carefully selected users should result in a generally acceptable product for internal use (Fig. 14.2). If possible, one of these users should be involved with general company management, otherwise the wider implications of the system may be overlooked. Where there is a suspicion that users may be hostile, it may be wise to enlist a hostile user in the development.

Unlike more conventional forms of software development (Mayhew *et al.*, 1989), iteration and rework are essential components of successful prototyping. I consider it a very serious danger signal if there is passive acceptance of the prototype by the users and no rework is demanded by them. This generally means not that the work is perfect, but that users are failing in the following ways:

- Users are not paying attention or are not having their attention attracted.
- Users do not have the time or opportunity to look carefully at the prototype.
- Users do not want to expose their own ignorance to their peers or managers.
- Users are afraid of criticizing the prototype, either because they are afraid of the prototypers or because they do not want to upset them.

The consequence of errors not being challenged rigorously at the early stage of development is the well-known multiplication effect of correcting

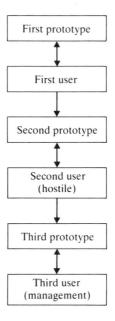

Figure 14.2   Stages of user evaluation

errors in the later stages of development (Boehm, 1981; Mason and Carey, 1983). It can be necessary with some users to make small mistakes deliberately or to provoke them in other ways. You should always remember that the earlier the problems are exposed, the easier they are to fix.

14.4   Implementation with teams

Prototyping can be carried out by teams of prototypers (Boehm *et al.*, 1984; Mayhew *et al.*, 1989). Team prototyping is a much more difficult exercise than individual prototyping. I would not recommend it as a first experience for organizations evaluating prototyping.

The following are some of the problem areas of team prototyping:

- Controlling changes that affect the overall development effort (Mayhew *et al.*, 1989).
- Decomposition of the development into modules that can be prototyped efficiently (Luqi and Berzine, 1988).
- Integration of the modules into a working product.

Prototyping depends a good deal on being able to effect rapid change in the software under development. These changes could, however, affect other developers in a large project. One aspect in which much care and coordination is required in team programming is that of the database design. If prototypers are permitted to make changes to the database without proper control, then other prototypers may be affected. Mayhew *et al.* (1989) suggest that classification of the nature of changes required (e.g. cosmetic, local, or global) is an important means of ensuring control and coordination of the prototyping team.

If the prototype is large enough to require a team effort, then careful decomposition of the project is needed in advance. This requirement reproduces the chicken-or-egg dilemma of conventional software development: that of not knowing the problem sufficiently well to analyse it until it has been implemented. There is a lot of intuition (Shandle, 1989), skill, experience, and luck needed to decompose large projects effectively. I suggest that large developments should be decomposed into modules that are small enough to permit prototyping on a one-to-one basis, i.e. one developer to one user. Carefully defined interfaces between modules (Boehm, 1987) permits modular software development without the need for extensive personal interaction.

The traditional-style approach for team prototyping would be to decompose the problem into modules and to develop the modules in parallel (Fig. 14.3). Integration of the modules should either be addressed on a frequent incremental basis (e.g. daily) or as part of a careful design of clearly defined interfaces between the prototype modules. The integrated product, in either case, should be evaluation often with the users, both as individual modules and as a whole. Failure to do so is likely to result in major integration problems towards the end of the development.

Because of the problems of developing software modules successfully in parallel, serious consideration should be given to the feasibility of serial modular development (Fig. 14.4). Serial development obviously implies an extended delivery date for the full system. In serial development, development of modules should be based on delivering the most needed functions first, if possible. A major advantage of this development style is that a smaller number of staff are required and management overheads may be reduced significantly. A possible problem, however, could be loss of focus during a very long development.

14.5 Integration

Prototypes being developed in conjunction with other systems are almost certain to share common data. Changes in the prototype database could affect other systems. The traditional way of controlling this problem is to permit only a database administrator (DBA) to make changes to the database. While this approach is unquestionably effective in preventing unauthorized changes, it can slow prototype development, especially at the early phases, to an intolerable rate.

One way this problem can be addressed is by employing local copies of

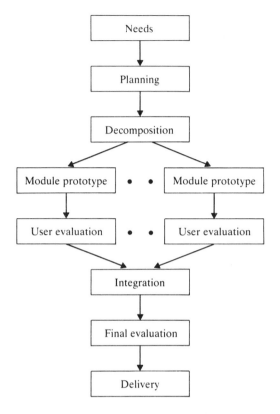

Figure 14.3   Parallel module development

the master database for each prototype. Prototypers are permitted to make changes freely to their local databases. Changes in the local databases can then be consolidated, harmonized, and documented on a regular and frequent basis by the DBA (Fig. 14.5). Unacceptable changes to the databases on a local basis will obviously necessitate rework on the prototype to incorporate these changes. This can be avoided to some degree by prototypers establishing an informal channel of communication with the DBA. If the DBA is unavailable, however, prototyping will not have to stop to wait for changes.

14.6   Final evaluation

A major problem with prototyping is supposed to be knowing when to stop. The phenomena of 'creeping excellence' and 'gold-plating' are only too well known (Boehm *et al.*, 1984) in all areas of software development. Stopping is where good judgement, a written plan, and strong management are needed

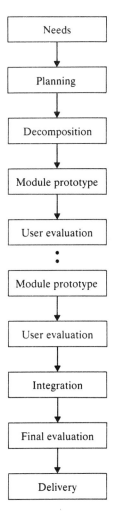

Figure 14.4   Serial modular prototyping

to decide when 'enough is enough'. An essential feature of prototyping, whether done by individuals or by teams, is that software is evaluated by users. This also is true of the final prototype. The granularity of evaluation depends on, to a large part, the availability and patience of the users doing the evaluation.

Reasonable expectations for the finished prototype are that it:

- Accurately reflects total user and organizational needs, even if these were not perceived at the beginning of development.
- Has appropriate, accurate, and efficient functions and algorithms.

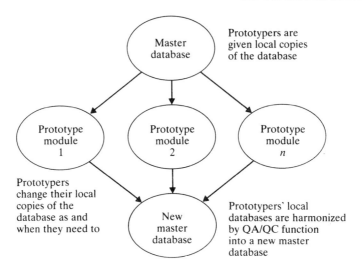

Figure 14.5 Harmonizing the master database

- Has a suitably finished appearance to the user and is easy to use, both in the long and short term.
- Is completed within any absolutely necessary time-scales and to budget allocation.
- Is in a reasonable condition, in terms of internal quality and document-ation, to be maintained for its expected lifetime.

A good sign of a successful implementation is that users are clamouring to use the prototype at this stage. Premature delivery can, however, lead to problems and disappointments (Ince, 1988). In the plan for the prototype, there should be procedures specified for determining that the implement-ation is complete. It is wise to stick to these procedures. Formal sign-off by those authorized to do so in the plan should be sought to reduce political problems later if the prototype should prove unsuccessful in any way.

14.7   Delivering prototypes

Delivery is the process of converting an implemented prototype into a target system. The enjoyable part of prototyping is now finished from the pro-grammer's viewpoint. From this point on, management may be pressing for early delivery and 'computing-hostile' users may be meeting the prototype for the first time: this is where things can go very wrong, very quickly.

Delivering an evolutionary prototype to a small population of expert users as a stand-alone target system usually requires little additional effort beyond implementation. If agreed beforehand, documentation can be word of mouth, informal training, and maintenance *ad hoc*. In this case, the prototype remains a prototype all its life. The important thing here is that the developer is likely to be available during the life of the software or, at least, during the first part of its life. There are few organizations, however, in which this would be an acceptable form of delivery.

Successful delivery of an evolutionary prototype to a wider, less expert audience or delivering a target system from a throw-away prototype is more difficult. Here, the prototype must become a more or less conventional system:

- User and internal documentation and training must be prepared and delivered.
- The system must be integrated with existing systems and data or, if partial prototype, embedded within a system.
- The system must be robust in the sense of being able to handle unexpected data, inexpert users, and deliberate abuse.
- The system must perform as expected, within the given hardware constraints.
- Maintenance must be able to be carried out on a formal, controlled, and guaranteed basis after delivery.

14.8   The activities of delivery

In many applications, some prototype delivery activities (Fig.14.6) can take place in parallel. Documentation is usually insensitive to positioning, providing that this is done before the end of the project. The delivery activities, of course, may result in modification of the prototype itself as difficulties present themselves. It is clear, therefore, that minimizing the possibility of reimplementation in the delivery stage will save a lot of time and effort in prototyping.

14.9   Achieving delivery

Prototyping greatly helps the delivery of documentation and training. For example, documenting a system that exists is bound to be a much more straightforward process than documenting a system that does not exist. Print-outs of screens can be produced easily for incorporation and early documentation can be evaluated by users of the prototype. Similarly, training is made easier: courses can be quickly prepared and training can commence in advance of delivery. The latter aspect is a very significant advantage.

The widespread perception of success about PCs should give some strong hints about documentation. The emphasis in prototyping should be upon happy users. 'Bright and cheerful' documentation will make many users and their managers happy, just by being there. Remember, too, that if your system is to be successful, i.e. long-lived, it will need documentation for generations of users who were not trained by developing the prototype. Good user

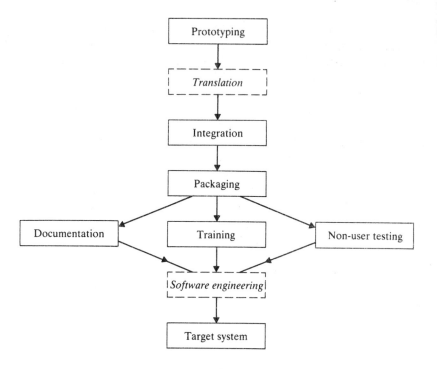

Figure 14.6   Activities of delivery

documentation is essential, and it is likely to be helpful to use a prototyping approach towards developing this.

I consider testing and final packaging to be essential steps in the prototyping process to achieve robustness. User evaluation of prototypes is not sufficiently testing to ensure robustness. Rigorous testing (Kopetz, 1976) of software internals by computing staff is essential. Packaging the prototype to provide adequate data input validation, help, and other expected aspects of the human–computer interface (HCI) is essential. Prototyping should, however, be able to resolve many of the HCI aspects of the application (Chap. 12).

Performance and integration are major difficulties in crossing the boundary between prototyping and delivery. Integration can be made easier by consideration, at the earliest stages, of the function of the prototype within the wider context of the business and all its systems. It may not be possible, however, to determine performance until delivery time. Final resolution of performance and integration can only be addressed by choosing either:

- A throw-away prototyping strategy that permits translation of the prototype into a more efficient and easily integrated form.
- Prototyping tools suitable to create efficient evolutionary prototypes with suitable interfaces.

Once the target system has been delivered, maintenance must begin. Effective maintenance is largely a matter of good management and a suitable prototyping strategy. Prototyping should have a positive effect on maintenance, since better quality software is likely to have resulted in the first place (Boehm *et al.*, 1984).

Maintenance of evolutionary prototypes is straightforward (Fig. 14.7). Changes are made directly to the prototype. The only real problems involve making sure that users know that changes have been made and of not 'breaking' the working system while maintaining it.

If a throw-away prototyping strategy is adopted, there remains the consideration of how to treat the prototype within the maintenance cycle (Fig. 14.8). One possibility is to continue to maintain the prototype as a source for the target system and to maintain it, rather than the target system. This is, for all intents and purposes, evolutionary prototyping, although the conversion must be repeated for every maintenance delivery.

The other possibility is to abandon the prototype after the first translation (Fig. 14.9). This is true throw-away prototyping. The translated program or new source must, of course, be in a form that can be maintained.

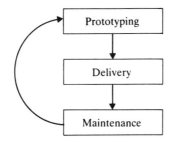

Figure 14.7 Evolutionary prototype maintenance

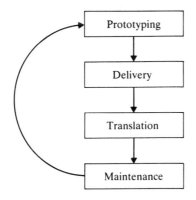

Figure 14.8 Throw-away prototype maintenance

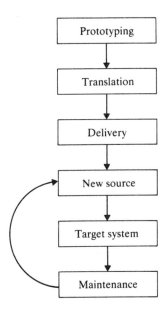

Figure 14.9   True throw-away prototype maintenance

The merits of any approach to maintaining prototypes tend to be individual to each application, each organization, and the prototyping tools employed (Mason and Carey, 1983). Maintenance of evolutionary prototypes excludes the possibility of introducing errors during translation and the cost of translation. On the other hand, an inefficient evolutionary prototype used by a large number of people or over a long period of time can cost a great deal of money.

Evolutionary prototyping has substantial benefits in the delivery phase. In spite of the potential problems, I think that it is reasonable practice to attempt to deliver evolutionary prototypes, if these are at all acceptable to the organization. Evaluate the evolutionary prototype carefully to see what are the implications of running it without translation. If it proves more expensive to run the prototype, as is, than it is to translate it, then translate it into a more efficient form.

14.10   Prototyping and databases

In my experience, most conventional business computer applications (or applications for other types of organizations) consist of three main components:

- Database.
- Data entry and editing.
- Reports and output.

In general, the most critical of these components, from a technical perspective, is the database (Jordan *et al.*, 1989). From the viewpoint of the day-to-day users, however, data entry is the most important. Management is likely to be seriously interested only in the reports of the application. If the database is designed properly, the rest of the applications development is essentially cosmetic (Mayhew *et al.*, 1989), even if it is not necessarily done rapidly. Getting users to validate database design completely, without prototyping, can be an exceedingly difficult task.

Evaluating the database fields is relatively easy. Data entry screens are created and presented to users; this first exposure usually elicits a flurry of criticisms. These criticisms are related to the absence of data fields that the users neglected to tell the prototyper about. The 'Gee, you left out the pig-flying-by-on-a-Thursday date. I would've thought anyone would have known about that!' type of dialogue should be a familiar one to every software developer. The difference between prototypers and conventional software developers is that the prototypers hear about missing fields at the start of the project. The conventional developers hear about them when they think the project is finished.

The most critical aspect of the design of the database is the structure. Using the relational paradigm, structure is the relationship between tables and the provision of fields that act as keys. Fortunately, by creating data entry screens from the database and getting users to enter real data at the earliest possible opportunity, it may be possible to verify most of the important database structures.

A warning is in order about prototyping and data structures. In my experience, while users know the data fields needed in the database, they may lack an appreciation of data structure. They even may have serious misapprehensions about it. Management generally has a better appreciation of data structure, providing the right person can be located. Therefore, it is important to attempt to involve both user and management in discussions about the database structure, even though it may prove difficult to do so from a communication point of view. Prototyping, however, is not a design tool. It will help elicit and evaluate data structures but it will not, in itself, reveal them.

If there is no real reason for exposing the database structure to the users, however, don't do it. If you feel you must show non-technicians the database structure, the best advice I can give is to try to keep database discussions as simple and as non-technical as possible. Do not bore the audience with displays of your technical virtuosity. The other tactic is to try to create a prototype of the full database at the earliest possible opportunity. This prototype should expose as many of the key data fields and their relationships to the user as possible.

It may be instructive to mention that in the last two prototypes in which I have been involved, it was necessary to alter radically the database structure after the first try. This involved completely scrapping the original work. Fortunately, the originals were only skeleton prototypes of the data structure, otherwise the amount of rework that would have been necessary later would have been very great.

14.11   Discussion

There is no 'best practice' yet established for the way of actually prototyping. In many ways, this may be beneficial since organizations can devise practices for themselves that are most suitable. The practice of prototyping requires a considerable amount of thought, however, and there are numerous possible approaches. Other than for large developments, carried out in parallel, I am not convinced that any particular approach to prototyping will be markedly successful over any other. What is most important is that the prototyping team has good users, prototypers, and managers.

15
Tools for prototyping

Conventional, well-accepted, and readily available software tools represent the least risk and lowest cost for prototyping in conventional organizations. Evaluation of the suitability of conventional software tools for prototyping must take several quantitative and qualitative factors into account:

- Functionality inherent to the tool, exclusive of its ability to import other functions. For example, in most installations, database access will be essential, but database functions may not be provided by the candidate tool. Evaluation of function requires a knowledge of the functions required by the organization.
- Development speed is an important aspect of making prototyping economical and effective. This can be evaluated by various benchmarks.
- Deliverability is the aggregate of features that permit the target system to be produced from the prototype. These factors were discussed in the previous chapter.
- Maintenance of the prototype, both rectification and enhancement, may be necessary. The prototyping tool should not impede effective maintenance. This aspect was discussed in the previous chapter.
- The prototyping tools themselves and the target systems produced must be effective within the business. Business effectiveness was defined earlier.

15.1 Conventional prototyping tools

To provide some flavour of prototyping with conventional tools, I have devised a very simple demonstration application. In spite of the triviality of the application, it shows many of the limitations and properties of each tool. The specification of the demonstration application is as follows:

- Input two numbers, of unspecified resolution.
- Output the sum of the two values.
- Save the two original values on disk without erasing earlier values.
- User interface should need little instruction or documentation to use application.

15.2 Compiled high-level languages

Compiled high-level languages (HLLs) or third-generation languages (3GLs), such as PASCAL (Boehm *et al.*, 1984), can be employed for prototyping. I have prototyped and delivered major systems (e.g. over 5000 lines of source program) in BASIC PLUS TWO (Smith and Lador, 1984) and in C (Kernigan and Ritchie, 1978). There is no reason why successful prototypes cannot be produced in any HLL, including such 'heavyweight' languages such as ADA, COBOL, or PL/1.

Prototypes implemented in compiled HLLs have virtually unlimited functionality, low development speed, good deliverability, average maintainability, and high cost effectiveness. Fast compilation, good debugging facilities, and availability of libraries of high-level functions (e.g. database access, windows, graphics) are important features to evaluate. Most HLLs are standardized and implementations adhere to them. Workstations or well-equipped personal computers are often an economical means of providing an efficient development enviroment.

Almost any type or size of application can be prototyped and delivered in a compiled HLL, given enough time or a good tool set. The level of technical skill required for prototyping effectively in compiled HLLs is very high. Most computer systems already have compilers and delivered target systems may incur no replication cost. There is little risk of adoption, other than the relatively low speed of development and the traditional difficulties of maintaining HLL programs.

The following is a source program, in C, for the sample application:

```
main ( )
{
float first, second;          /* define */
FILE *output;                 /* variables */

output=fopen("data","a");     /* open file */

printf("First number?");      /* input numbers */
scanf("%f", &first);
printf("Second number?");
scanf("%f", &second);
printf("The sum is %f\n", first + second);    /* print sum */
fprintf("%f\n%f\n", first, second);           /* save to disk */
}                                              /* end program */
```

This C program has little robustness. There are no error-trapping on input or file operations. The program will fail on error, give a cryptic error message, at best, and return to the operating system. The HCI of this program consists of simple, scrolled input prompts and no opportunity to edit after entering the numbers. Improving robustness and the HCI (e.g. detecting null values, range checking, help) would be a major programming undertaking, even with appropriate tool sets (e.g. CURSES, X). Note that comments are required to make the program readable for those not acquainted with C.

Developing compiled HLL prototypes can be tedious, even with good facilities (Figure 15.1). It can take a long time to eliminate apparently simple syntactical errors in HLLs. C makes the generation of fatal syntax errors (e.g. forgetting the '&' before the variables in the scanf statement) easy. I recently had an experience in which it took four hours to find a missing comment terminator (i.e. */) in a statement. Neither the compiler nor any of the many UNIX utilities were any help. I finally spotted it by reading the print-out. A good debugger is an essential feature of rapid prototype development in HLLs.

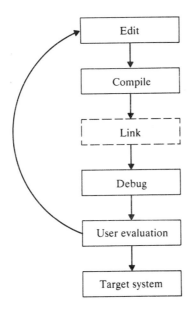

Figure 15.1   Typical compiled language prototyping cycle

15.3 Interpreted high-level languages

Interpreted HLLs, such as APL (Tavalato and Vincena, 1984), BASIC, or MUMPS, can be employed for prototyping (Hekmatpour and Ince, 1986). I have developed and delivered at least a dozen prototypes in interpreted HLLs (Smith, 1986); however, none of the systems were as large as those produced in compiled HLLs.

Interpreted HLLs tend to have moderate to good functionality, medium to high development speed, medium to high deliverability, and medium to high business effectiveness. Maintainability can be worse than with compiled HLLs. Features to evaluate are functionality (e.g. database and external function access), performance, existence of a compiler version of the HLL, target computer availability, and unit cost. Most interpreted HLLs have a standard but these are often extended or ignored.

Many computer systems already have HLL interpreters, usually BASIC. Target systems may require an interpreter; this can affect replication costs. The amount of skill required for programming is less than for compiled HLLs but is still high. It should be possible to implement most small to medium-sized applications effectively in interpreted languages. Larger applications may prove more difficult to implement because of inherently lower performance (Gries, 1971), difficulty of maintenance, lack of modularity, no access to external functions, and restricted availability of suitable interpreters on larger computer systems.

The following is a BASIC source program for the sample application:

```
10   OPEN "data" FOR APPEND AS FILE #1
20   INPUT "First number"; FIRST
30   INPUT "Second number"; SECOND
40   PRINT "The sum is"; FIRST + SECOND
50   PRINT #1, FIRST
60   PRINT #1, SECOND
```

The robustness of this program is slightly better than that of the C program since incorrect input will automatically cause a repeat of the relevant INPUT statement. The program will still fail if there is a file error, although it will return to BASIC instead of the operating system. There is no improvement of the HCI and the amount of programming is similar to that of C. Worse still, there is a good chance that incorporating tools or program modules might not be as easy. In this type and size of application, performance would not be appreciably slower than for the C program.

Developing this interpreted BASIC program is straightforward and rapid. The BASIC interpreter is invoked from the operating system and the source is typed using the built-in editor. The program is run and debugged from within BASIC. Syntactical errors may be trapped by the editor and some BASIC interpreters have good debug facilities. Larger programs are less easy to develop in older BASIC interpreters because of primitive subroutine and function creation facilities (i.e. lack of modularity).

15.4 Tool sets

Tool sets, such as the operating system UNIX, have been cited as being suitable for prototyping (Hekmatpour and Ince, 1986; Ince, 1988; Riddle, 1984; Schnupp, 1984). UNIX is particularly useful because the tools can be connected rapidly using the shell. I have employed UNIX for implementing prototypes, one quite large in terms of function, but have never been able to deliver such a system successfully.

Prototypes developed using UNIX utilities and the shell (i.e. the operating system procedural language) tend to have moderate functionality, medium development speed, medium to high deliverability, and medium to high cost effectiveness. UNIX-based prototypes can prove slow to develop because of the lack of good debugging facilities in the shell. Most UNIX tools are not well suited for non-technical end-users and this limits 'packageability' severely. Performance of prototypes created from UNIX tools can be disappointing. Delivery will prove difficult unless the target computer also employs UNIX.

The simple application implemented in the UNIX shell language (Bourne, 1978) is:

```
echo "First number?\c"
read $first
echo "Second Number?\c"
read $second
echo "The sum is \c"
expr $first + $second          # add and output the numbers
echo $first >> data            # append first number
echo $second >> data           # append second number
```

The robustness of this shell script is even worse than that of the C program since non-numerical input is not trapped and may produce unexpected results. The classical joke in UNIX is to type your name into the shell and see how much damage it causes. Floating-point numbers cannot be evaluated without creating a special software tool. The HCI is similar to that of C and BASIC; improving the HCI would take a special program. Even in this simple application, performance would be noticeably slower than either C or BASIC programs.

Developing this shell script is easy, if you know UNIX. An editor must be used to enter the script and is shell invoked afterwards from the operating system. Debug facilities are primitive and mainly of the trial-and-error variety. This application does not show the shell at its best. It is more impressive when invoking much larger scale functions, such as complex file sorts and joins (i.e. relating one file to another). I have, however, found the user interface and slow performance to be a serious impediment to delivery.

15.5 Database management systems

Database management systems (DBMSs), such as dBASE, INFORMIX, INGRES, or ORACLE, can be used to prototype most applications in the commercial domain (Dearnley and Mayhew, 1984; Livesey, 1984; Parbst, 1984). It is difficult to overstress the importance of data to almost all commercial applications (Jordan *et al.*, 1989; Kreplin, 1984). Thus, a software tool that operates in this area is probably the most effective prototyping tool available at present. I have implemented many prototypes and have delivered at least six large evolutionary prototypes in various DBMSs (e.g. DATATRIEVE, INFORMIX, and ORACLE) within commercial organizations.

Prototypes developed in DBMSs tend to have good functionality, high development speed, low to excellent deliverability, and low to high business effectiveness. The functionality of DBMSs tend to be adequate for most applications, although extensibility of function can be poor. There are no standards for DBMSs although many are based on the SQL or CODASYL data retrieval languages (Date, 1977). Adoption of a DBMS is a major strategic decision that should be taken with great care and within the full context of the business. The cost of a DBMS for a large computer system can be high, e.g. £100 000 for a 100-user system in the UK.

The speed of development of DBMSs for most large and complex applications is probably about two orders of magnitude faster than an equivalent implementation in a HLL such as C, even C with a good tool set. The maintainability and deliverability of DBMS applications are of a similar degree. Sufficient skill to generate simple applications can be gained in a day's training or less, even by those without a technical background.

Deliverability and cost effectiveness are directly related to the availability of the chosen DBMS on the target computer. If the DBMS cannot be made available, then the prototype must be a throw-away. Otherwise, it is usually possible to construct rapidly large, well-packaged, scalable, easily maintained, well integrated, and highly deliverable prototypes using DBMSs. It is important to recognize that a DBMS provides automatically a practical and unambiguous interface to all data used or produced by the prototype. As a result, the problems of interfacing are greatly reduced when a DBMS is employed.

The demonstration of the simple application is for ORACLE (ORACLE, 1986), a typical DBMS. The DBMS approach is less straightforward to show than for the other tools because of the non-procedural nature of ORACLE. First, the database language SQL is invoked and the following command issued to create the database table, if the table does not exist already:

```
create table data
(
first__number        number              not null,
second__number       number              not null
);
```

Input to the database is through a screen created by a DBMS software tool (e.g. ORACLE, 1986), called the screen generator. The screen generator can produce a default screen in a minute or two (Fig. 15.2). The default screen permits full editing of both fields before calculation; null values cannot be entered. The screen also allows retrieval of all previous values. A few minutes more work will permit display of the sum of the two fields by attaching a function (an ORACLE trigger) to the screen:

```
select  :first__number +   :second__number into   :sum
```

Adding an even more elaborate HCI with help screens, full-range checking, and menus would be a matter of a few minutes effort in most DBMS products. Null and illegal values are prohibited within the definition of the two variables. Other programs requiring this data would access through the same DBMS mechanisms, using the same table and variable names.

The addition of the two values in the demonstration application shows a major technical limitation of DBMSs, however. First, the operation is not obvious without special ORACLE training. Secondly, if it had been a more complex mathematical function (e.g. trigonometry), it might not have been possible to do it in ORACLE at all. This is characteristic of DBMSs: when they are reluctant to perform a task, they simply do not do it. Worse still, it may prove possible to do it, but in a way that is exceedingly difficult to maintain. Extensibility permits most functions to be carried out in a fairly sensible way. Unfortunately, this is likely to slow development or lead to maintenance problems.

Similarly, the HCI of most DBMSs is more or less fixed. If the inherent

DATA		
First number	Second number	Sum of numbers

Figure 15.2 ORACLE screen

HCI is not adequate, then that DBMS may not be suitable for the application. Modification of the DBMS HCI is almost certain to add greatly to complexity, reduce performance, increase costs, and cause severe maintenance and familiarization problems.

15.6 Hybrid solutions

Unfortunately, not all applications can be implemented fully or sensibly in DBMSs. Many 3GLs do not have database functions embedded within the language. When this happens, it is necessary to create hybrid programs with DBMS functions. For example, a simple C program interfaced to ORACLE (ORACLE, 1985) would look something like this:

```
EXEC SQL BEGIN DECLARE SECTION:
    VARCHAR uid[20]:
    VARCHAR password[20]:
    char last_name[30]:
    char first_name[30]:
EXEC SQL END DECLARE SECTION:
EXEC SQL INCLUDE SQLCA:

main ( )
{       /* Application must log into ORACLE */
    strcpy(uid.arr, "SMITH"):
    strcpy(password.arr, "JUNK"):
    uid.len=strlen(uid.arr):
    password.len=strlen(password.arr):
    EXEC SQL WHENEVER SQLERROR STOP:
    EXEC SQL CONNECT :uid IDENTIFIED BY :password
    /* Now do the selection */
    EXEC SQL DECLARE C1 CURSOR FOR
            SELECT LAST_NAME, FIRST_NAME
            FROM ADDRESS WHERE LAST_NAME='Smith'
            ORDER BY FIRST_NAME:
    EXEC SQL OPEN C1:
    EXEC SQL WHENEVER NOT FOUND STOP:
    /* Print using C functions */
    for( ; ; ) /* Run until ORACLE aborts */
    {
    EXEC SQL FETCH C1 INTO : last_name, :first_name:
    printf("%s %s\n", :last_name, first_name):
    }
    EXEC SQL CLOSE C1:
    EXEC SQL WHENEVER SQLERROR CONTINUE:
    EXEC SQL COMMIT WORK RELEASE:
    exit(0):
} /*   End of the Program */
```

Not a pretty sight, is it? The hybrid program is neither quick to write nor easy to maintain.

Of course, in a totally 'raw' 3GL, such a database example might require many thousands of lines of program. This pure 3GL program would be even more difficult to read, write, and maintain than the hybrid ORACLE and C example above. It is not difficult for me to recommend very strongly the use of DBMSs whenever possible as conventional prototyping tools. I might even go so far, in many organizations, as to recommend not developing software at all if 3GL programming were to be required in the application.

15.7 Fourth-generation languages

Fourth-generation languages (4GLs) and very high-level languages (VHLLs) (Budde, 1984; Hekmatpour and Ince, 1986; Ince, 1989) are well-known software tool concepts. 4GLs are, however, far from being clearly defined (IT-STARTS, 1989a). 4GLs (Martin, 1984) appear to be the commercial manifestation of the concept of VHLLs, although not necessarily in agreement with the academic concept of VHLLs. In general, 4GLs have functionality similar to that of DBMSs. Many retain the conventional programming paradigm, however, and have additional functions, similar to those of conventional 3GLs. The combination of these features should eliminate the unattractive prospect of resorting to hybrid 3GL – DBMS solutions to solve the problems, often simple ones, that DBMSs alone cannot.

Fourth-generation languages are highly suitable software tools for prototyping (Boehm and Papaccio, 1988; Monckemeyer and Spitta, 1984). Their productivity can be three to six times greater than 3GLs (Boehm, 1987) or more (Jones, 1986). The major problem with 4GLs is that they are seen as being risky to adopt, because they have not yet gained any degree of standardization, nor is there even a clear market leader yet. Trained staff can be difficult to find and keep. 4GLs can be expensive to purchase and target system replication costs can be frighteningly high because of this. There are worries (Boehm, 1987), possibly unjustified (Bloor, 1989), about poor performance and interfacing. At present, small and medium-sized organizations could find these reservations about 4GLs daunting. Fortunately, many commercial DBMSs appear to be evolving rapidly into 4GL products.

15.8 Spreadsheets

Spreadsheets, such as Lotus 1-2-3 and Excel, have been employed by many, including myself, to create prototypes. Spreadsheets can be excellent prototyping tools because of their high functionality and excellent productivity (Jones, 1986) for mathematically oriented applications. Many spreadsheets produce high-quality graphical and report output and have some DBMS functions. The spreadsheet paradigm and user interface is one with which certain types of user relate easily. Prototypes developed using spreadsheets, however, tend to have restricted functionality, low to medium deliverability, poor maintainability, and medium to high business effectiveness.

Spreadsheets can prove to be rather dangerous in prototyping because they 'almost work'. Not all spreadsheets provide access to external functions or incorporate suitable databases. The spreadsheet paradigm is not capable of solving all classes of problem easily. Once the programmer reverts to complex spreadsheet macros, conventional programming is probably as efficient and likely to be more easily maintained. Poor overall performance, limited portability, and high replication costs of spreadsheets are features that should be evaluated carefully for the specific application. Packaging spreadsheets to be used by naïve end users can prove virtually impossible.

Generally, spreadsheets are likely to prove unsatisfactory tools for developers creating efficient, large-scale, deliverable, and maintainable prototypes. I have seen their restricted functionality, limited portability, and poor extendability lead developers into expensive technical 'blind alleys' when it has been attempted to deliver spreadsheet-based software to users. Spreadsheets are excellent throw-away prototyping tools, however, and can provide highly effective, short-term, stop-gap systems.

15.9   Screen editors and word processors

Simple screen editors can serve as powerful prototyping tools, especially for throw-away prototyping. They can be employed to produce simulated text and graphics input and output. Screens can be stored and coupled to simple animation programs to provide dynamic prototypes to users. Graphics editors, such as MacDraw, can be used to generate more complex prototypes in an application area in which prototyping is particularly valuable.

Word processing systems may have considerable function beyond simple editing. Many word processors contain modest database and report-generating capabilities. These may be employed to produce throw-away prototypes or can even be embedded into delivered systems. It is worth remembering, as well, that word processors and editors are complex software tools but ones with which many users feel entirely comfortable. As such, they provide a useful paradigm for developers. Since editors are unlikely to be perceived as capable of providing final systems, the danger of attempting to deliver prototypes based on them is limited.

15.10   Executable specifications

Executable specifications, such as ADS (Powell, 1987), HOS (Martin, 1984), VDM with PSN (Lamersdorf and Schmidt, 1984), automatic tool set assemblers (Luqi and Berzins, 1988), and computer-aided software engineering tools have been proposed as suitable tools for prototyping. In these tools, the prototype is generated from analysis and specification documentation (Bates, 1989).

These tools require a formal and precise specification language that is unlikely to have much meaning to the users. The benefit, of course, is that users do not need to understand this documentation, which is, in any event, needed for computing technologists. Executable specifications are still largely experimental (Luqi and Ketabchi, 1988) and, consequently, are excessively risky for adoption at this time.

15.11   Object-oriented languages

Object-oriented languages (OOLs), such as ADA, C++ (Stroustrup, 1986), or SIMULA (Birtwistle *et al.,* 1980), are similar to conventional (i.e. 3GL) languages. Their flexibility, data abstraction, overloading, and inheritance features (Scown, 1985), however, permit creation of higher-level functions and encourage greater software reusability (Fischer, 1989). These features are supposed to boost productivity (Maxwell, 1988) and maintainability, and could prove highly attractive to prototypers.

Object-oriented programming techniques are becoming widely accepted and can even be employed using conventional HLLs. The risk of adopting an OOL is low, particularly if one based on a conventional language is selected (e.g. ADA or C++). Standards appear to be evolving rapidly and the risk of adoption is likely to prove low. The cost of acquiring OOLs is not appreciably higher than that of conventional languages, although considerable training and familiarization may be required to exploit their features.

My own recent experience with the object-oriented language C++ (Zortech, 1986) is inconclusive. It took me about three days reading (Stroustrup, 1986) and experimenting to come to grips with it. Its similarity with C, which I had last used two years earlier, was a help. Using C++ and a tool set (Zortech, 1987), which I modified extensively, it took seven days to produce a 1500-line prototype of a fairly complex product. While this seems reasonable productivity, I am uncertain how much the object-oriented features helped. I might well have produced the same amount of work in C, but without the cost of three days of familiarization.

What is unclear at present is how much greater productivity OOLs provide than conventional HLLs. If their productivity is similar to that of DBMSs or 4GLs, then their adoption for prototyping should be considered. What must be kept in mind, however, is the typical need for database access and screen-painting facilities. If, on the other hand, they are only somewhat more productive than HLLs, organizations would be advised to consider investment in OOLs as a luxury that may not assist prototyping substantially.

15.12   Artificial intelligence languages and tools

Artificial intelligence (AI) languages, such as LISP or PROLOG (Leibrandt and Schnupp, 1984; Schnupp, 1984), and expert systems shells (Scown, 1985) can be employed for prototyping (Hekmatpour and Ince, 1986; Jordan *et al.*, 1989). The functionality, deliverability, maintainability, and cost effectiveness of AI languages are similar to those of conventional interpreted 3GLs. AI languages may be more functional than conventional languages in some respects (e.g. extensibility, inference mechanisms) but less functional in others (e.g. mathematical operations, database access).

Expert systems have been a particularly prominent manifestation of AI. Expert systems generators tend to be highly functional in terms of HCI and AI functions; most also permit escape to external functions. It is likely that part of the success of expert systems is related to a prototyping style of elicitation of expert knowledge from users and their emphasis on 'slick' HCI. As such, expert systems generators may be functionally suitable for general-purpose prototyping (Jordan *et al.*, 1989), even though their internal mechanisms may be exotic and their technical terminology arcane.

The risks associated with adoption of LISP or PROLOG for prototyping is low because these languages are well accepted and reasonably well standardized. Performance is generally similar to that of interpreted languages and there is a reasonably high degree of portability. Expert systems shells are more risky because they are unstandardized, proprietary products. Their portability is low and performance in large applications may prove disappointing. Although expert systems provide excellent HCIs, these may not be amenable to customization.

15.13   Other conventional software tools

Software tools not intended for software development, such as simulators (Floyd, 1984), editors (Ince, 1988), and graphics packages (MacDraw) can be employed to produce prototypes (Hekmatpour and Ince, 1986). I have seen even specialized computer-aided design (AutoCad) and geographical information systems (ArcInfo) employed to produce fairly elaborate prototypes. It is possible to use most software tools for prototype development, even if only as examples of what not to do. It is probable, however, that prototypes produced with software tools not intended for software development will be functionally incomplete, lack deliverability, and prove difficult to maintain.

15.14   Conclusion

The triviality of the simple application presented here, although useful enough, tends to favour primitive software development tools, such as 3GLs. In reality, most commercial applications require complex interactive database operations such as entering, searching, sorting, and manipulating complex database records. These types of operations can be easily handled by a database language, such as SQL, in a single statement, e.g.

```
select last_name, first_name
    from address where last_name='Smith'
    order by first_name
```

Even with tool sets that provide DBMS-type function, software complexity tends to be much greater with 3GLs than with using DBMSs to produce applications. Consequently, DBMSs would appear to be the most suitable type of conventional software tool for prototyping in the majority of business applications.

There are some conventional software tools that, perhaps unexpectedly, can be employed in an unconventional way to produce prototypes. These tools are primarily valuable for creating throw-away prototypes. They have the advantage of requiring no new investment and little, if any, training. Their use can have serious repercussions when they start to be used seriously.

There are also relatively new software tools that may be of value in prototyping or specially designed for this task. New software tools inherently represent a high risk to their adopters because of the uncertainty of their long-term acceptability and viability. Although potentially useful and possibly worth tracking, many new software tools are, at present, unlikely to meet the needs of prototyping within the domain of small to medium-sized organizations engaged in typical commercial data-processing applications.

Of all the unconventional software tools, fourth-generation languages appear to have the greatest potential to benefit prototyping in the long run. Their ability to descend to third-generation language function, combined with database management system capability, makes them powerful tools for prototyping. Where organizations can accept the risks associated with early adoption, 4GLs are to be recommended for prototyping.

16

Prototyping and the human–computer interface

The issue of human-computer interfaces (HCIs), man–machine interfaces (MMIs), and graphical user interfaces (GUIs) has become an important one in computing (Hix, 1989). There is also a long-standing emphasis on HCIs in prototyping, which has partly come about because of the widespread need for prototyping to resolve HCI issues (Fischer, 1989) rather than through any inherent association between the two subjects (Bates, 1989).

Many of the issues of prototyping can be resolved through good HCIs and vice versa (Heckel, 1984). Prototypers should also remember that much of the perception of success of PC software is achieved by a high degree of 'user friendliness', no matter how facile.

16.1 Similar problem domains

From a software development viewpoint, HCI development and prototyping share many of the same problems:

- Complex, unquantified user needs and demands.
- Unsuitable software implementation tools.
- Inadequate software development methodologies.

The success of systems such as the Apple Macintosh can be attributed in large part to its outstanding HCI/GUI. From the software development point of view, use of an effective and consistent HCI technology could solve many of the problems of applications:

- The effectiveness of user interaction may be improved through provision of technical features.
- Users may require less time for training, familiarization, and support.
- User error rates may be reduced.

- As much as 50 per cent of typical systems may consist of HCI functions (B. A. Myers, 1989); packaged HCI solutions could save much of that expense.

Good HCIs may also be capable of improving the political interaction between users and developers:

- User satisfaction may be improved because they perceive that their needs are being addressed.
- There is a greater 'comfort factor' from having online help and assistance.
- Users may appreciate the 'technical machismo' of modern interfaces, especially GUIs.

16.2   HCI problems

In spite of the obvious value of good HCIs to mainstream computing applications, I have reservations about the subject, especially where GUIs are concerned. These reservations are not eased by the fervent 'hype' and 'one solution for everything' attitudes that are unfortunately prevalent in the literature about the subject. My reservations about excessive emphasis on HCI/GUI technology in custom software development are the following:

- Greater software complexity is certain to result, particularly if the HCI/GUI is embedded within the application (B. A. Myers, 1989). This is likely to lead to higher costs and earlier maintenance critical mass for custom software.
- Much technical skill is required to produce effective, efficient HCIs/GUIs (Fischer, 1989; B. A. Myers, 1989). Internal software development operations are already short of skilled and effective programmers. Their budgets are unlikely to be increased. Contention for resources may result in few applications being satisfied in favour of providing cosmetic features.
- Trivialization of computer applications. Excessive emphasis on HCIs/GUIs may distract users and programmers from fully developing the part of the application that is intended to profit the business.
- Loss of performance and portability. The highly interactive nature of modern GUIs requires considerable computer power and significant use of specific features to a particular computer and operating system.
- Higher hardware costs (e.g. workstations, PCs, colour, mouse, HCI/GUI software). The need for greater performance and specialized hardware for HCIs/GUIs increases computing cost substantially.
- There are no formulas or techniques that guarantee the creation of an effective HCI (B. A. Myers, 1989; Thomas and Kellogg, 1989). Lower productivity can result when HCIs are inappropriate (e.g. mouse interaction can be slow when keyboard operations are mixed; the WIMP para-

digm may prove inappropriate in some applications; poor use of colours can cause operator fatigue). Tufte's (1983) excellent treatment of graphics warns about the problems of graphical 'chartjunk'; this warning is also applicable to HCIs.

- Substitution of proper education and training for HCIs. The best HCI interface is a well-trained and adaptable human being. A week's investment in training may achieve more than the most attractive HCI and cost a great deal less.

Unfortunately, good HCI characteristics and long-term value may not prove to be compatible. For example, few people would claim that the HCI of the UNIX screen editor vi is an attractive one, and I certainly found it exceedingly difficult to learn. The commands are cryptic and the documentation confusing. The command mode, counter-intuitively, takes precedence over the editing mode. I often tell people, with some truth, that it took me two years to learn vi properly. Once learned, however, I found vi's efficiency, power of function, and speed of use to be superior to all other editors or word processors I have ever used. What this may suggest is that easy familiarity is not necessarily a good guarantee of the long-term suitability of software. Of course, this story also could simply prove the perversity of individual tastes. Even that conclusion tends to support some of my worries.

It should come as no surprise that the most critical HCI factors are human ones (Thomas and Kellogg, 1989):

- User experience, bias, and pre-familiarity.
- User attitude towards technology.
- User motivation.

Pre-familiarity may perhaps be the most important aspect of the HCI of a software product (Heckel, 1984), even if its academic HCI aspects are poor. For example, the QWERTY keyboard layout has its origins in mechanical design. It is thought not to be the most efficient layout, but it is adequate for those trained to use it. The cost of moving away from the QWERTY layout would probably far exceed any benefits to be gained. Another example of a debatable HCI is Lotus 1-2-3. I always find the Lotus HCI paradigm difficult to remember and slow to use. Those who know no other software or like it for personal reasons, however, prefer it above all other software interfaces. As a result, this has become an important HCI style. Familiarity and long-term stability (Newman, 1989) of the HCI seem to be highly important aspects of HCI effectiveness.

16.3   Discussion

I suspect that the factors involved in HCIs are too personal and experience-based to be formulated easily. This view appears to be substantiated in some HCI literature (Fischer, 1989; B. A. Myers, 1989). Even the HCI expectations of users will mutate with experience and changing application needs. I am sceptical of there being anything approaching an optimum HCI. This is particularly true in custom software where applications are, almost by definition, unique.

The need for attractive cosmetic appearance and rapid user familiarization is unquestionably important for the package software industry to produce 'friendly' products. These features are needed to induce customers to buy products and to be satisfied with them during the first few days of use. It is also important that the customer does not require any expensive training and support. Long-term effectiveness is likely to be secondary. Most buyers will never reach the point where the software they buy is important to the operation of their business.

Custom software for internal computing operations, on the other hand, does not necessarily need a high degree of cosmestic appeal or rapid user familiarization to be successful. The software should be sufficiently important to the operation of the business that users do not require artificial stimulation to use it. If it is not, the organization should seriously consider if the software really is needed enough to offset the risks of producing it. Support and training should be expected for custom software. Excessive emphasis on introducing leading-edge HCI techniques into custom software could be contrary to actual user experience and expectations and excessively expensive to provide. For example, if users are familiar and comfortable with the character-based style of Lotus 1-2-3 on a normal PC keyboard, will a more expensive WIMP-based GUI really be more appropriate?

It seems impossible, at present, to formulate HCI needs. In the end, they may prove to be based largely on past user experience. It is clear that evolution is the most successful approach to HCIs, and prototyping is likely to remain the most appropriate means of producing effective HCIs in custom software.

Part Five
Conclusion

In many ways, prototyping is an exceedingly difficult software development approach to advocate. Prototyping is not so much a clearly defined method for software development as an attitude towards software development. The principles of prototyping are simple: substitute or augment the analytical approach with iterative development involving the users. The essential tools are technically competent staff with a strong desire to produce software that users want and need. Prototyping is such a simple concept, yet is is one seemingly so difficult for software developers to accept.

My advocacy of prototyping is made even more difficult by my recognition that rigorous proof in its favour is unlikely. The lack of rigorous proof for any other software approach is little consolation. What I do believe is that prototyping is a logical and pragmatic approach to software development. There is evidence and experience pointing to its effectiveness, given suitable staff and management. Prototyping is also a benign approach: it requires little investment and its adoption is not irreversible.

There seems little question that prototyping can be incorporated within traditional and software engineering approaches. Compromise is possible, but approaches to compromise are not yet well established. Confrontation and polarization appear to be easier and more fashionable. All of the vagaries, problems, and uncertainties make it difficult to stand up and thump out a simple, direct message about how to adopt, practise, and manage prototyping. Perhaps that is because there is no simple message.

The objections that prototyping raise within the software development profession suggest to me that many of the profession's problems are those of attitude. Without a positive change of attitude in all those involved in software development, prototyping cannot help overcome the problems. Attitudes are difficult to transfer because they are necessarily vague. I recommend to you, 'involve the users', 'work in small teams', 'choose good tools', and the like. But just saying these is not enough to effect technology transfer. These principles are already well known in all development approaches. The problem is a well-known one; 'golden rules' are all too often heard, but not practised.

Prototyping and organizations

Prototyping is an approach that is readily applicable to many aspects of in-house, commercial data-processing applications development (Boar, 1984). I believe that prototyping is likely to be more appropriate and easier to adopt in small and medium-sized organizations than in large ones. This is because of the following properties of smaller organizations:

- They are less able to sustain full-time, specialized, and 'unproductive' software development staff such as software engineers, librarians, and analysts. These staff are required in the traditional and software engineering approaches.
- They have budgets that may be too small to support the adoption of high-cost software engineering technology, such as CASE, or to sustain widespread use of labour-intensive formal methods.
- They have smaller computing operations and are likely to have less rigid 'software bureaucracies'. Smaller operations may be able to take up a major change such as prototyping more easily. Leadership and priority approaches to management are more likely to be accepted and succeed than in larger companies.
- They should find it easier, because of their smaller size, to gain full user and highest-level management support for prototyping in a reasonable time.
- They may need the improved development quality and efficiency of prototyping more than larger organizations.

Even the best prototype developers and users must have good management and genuine leadership. Effective management can ensure that prototyping does not become an excuse for 'playing computers', sloppy work, lack of planning, or never-ending projects. Strong-willed, politically astute, and well-informed management, at all levels, must be exercised to achieve maximum success in prototyping.

Throw-away and evolutionary prototyping

At one time, I held the view that all prototypes should be of the throw-away variety (Smith, 1981). My attitude then was mainly based on the premise of inadequate prototyping tools and, frankly, timidity in putting forward such a radical proposal as employing prototypes 'for real'. This view and its reasons still have considerable validity. Throw-away prototyping should be used where performance or deliverability are highly important or where unsuitable prototyping tools must be employed, for whatever reason. Throw-away prototyping also appears to be the most sensible style of prototyping within environments that remain strongly aligned towards the traditional and software engineering approaches.

I no longer feel, however, that throw-away prototyping is necessarily the only option available. The efficiency of database management systems (DBMSs) now makes evolutionary prototyping practical in some cases. For example, in information management applications (Kammersgaard and Munkegade, 1984), where DBMSs can be employed totally, evolutionary prototyping may provide more rapid and less expensive results than any other development approach. If necessary, reverse engineering may be applied at the end of development to produce appropriate documentation.

Evolutionary prototyping seems especially appropriate in small and medium-sized organizations. The technical caveat I would give about them is that reasonable maintenance, coexistence, and interface with other systems must be planned and achieved. The political caveat is that considerable managerial and political skill is required to gain acceptance, especially with computer staff, of such a radical approach to software development.

Recommendations

I recommend that all organizations that produce software should evaluate prototyping seriously. Organizations should evaluate prototyping both as a stand-alone development approach and as an adjunct to the current software development approach. If suitable, prototyping should be harmonized with and embedded into the adopting organization's view of software development. Organizations should also consider seriously the role for evolutionary prototyping within their operations.

I also recommend strongly that all prototyping should be planned carefully and a brief written specification produced for every prototype developed. There should also be a written statement of the function of the prototype within the context of the business and systems of the organization. Organizations, even small ones, should produce a written overall computing strategy on a regular basis, probably no less than once every three years. Prototyping must be done within the context of this organizational computing strategy if it is to produce maximum success.

Appropriate and familiar software tools can facilitate prototyping substantially (Jordan *et al.*, 1989). Tools may be essential for an effective evolutionary prototyping approach. The DBMS probably represents the most business effective and least risky prototyping tool in the domain of commercial applications. The evolution of DBMSs into fourth-generation languages (4GLs) is likely to be the most acceptable future direction for commercial prototyping tools. Consequently, those involved in prototyping should keep themselves up to date on the progress of 4GLs. No matter what prototyping tools are employed, there should be a conscious attempt to reuse as much software, including designs and documentation, as possible.

Most computer applications are only valuable for the data that they produce or manipulate. Interfacing prototypes with the data and functions of other systems in the organization can be critical, and this must, therefore, be a major technical and operational consideration during prototype planning, implementation, and delivery. An appropriate DBMS can provide an excellent solution to most problems of applications interfacing in the commercial programming domain. The DBMS, therefore, may be seen to be a critical component in the adoption and practice of prototyping.

There is a fairly consistent view in the literature that prototyping teams should be kept small (Boehm *et al.*, 1984). I would go even further and recommend reducing prototyping teams to one developer and one user whenever possible, even if the elapsed time to completion is longer. Larger systems, if absolutely necessary, should be decomposed into 'one-to-one' sized components that exhibit as little interdependence as possible.

My final recommendations about prototyping concern people. Effective prototyping relies on software developers with good technical and people skills. Find these developers, train them, educate them, and do your best to keep them. Receptive, knowledgeable, and educated users, including general management, are also critical for success in prototyping. Users and managers must know their own subject and be realistic in their expectations about what computers can and cannot do. They must be prepared to speak up and tell the computer people what they want done.

Conclusion

In many ways, I am not so much putting the case in this book for prototyping, as reacting against wasteful, mechanistic, inappropriate, and unimaginative management styles and software development approaches. The traditional and software engineering approaches have simply not proven adequately successful, in many cases, in achieving their goals. As well as appearing to be seriously flawed in their base assumptions, they seem to widen the gap between users and developers, their benefits appear intangible, and they may increase software development cost. I believe that those who support these approaches should appreciate these criticisms and answer them, if they can.

The software development profession appears to have put itself into an especially difficult position with software engineering. By considering itself a part of 'big engineering', the profession seems to have locked itself into the heroic tradition of big projects in which no mistakes can be made. Here, all the carefully designed and machined components are brought together, at the last moment, with split-second timing. A bridge must work first time and keep on working; there are no second chances in a moon shot.

Programs are not bridges or moon shots, however, nor is all engineering of the heroic mould. In most business software there is no need to escalate risk and cost just to be able to have the software work right from the start. Software is infinitely malleable and most routine business developments are not life or business threatening. Usually, there is plenty of margin for gradual, cautious implementation in software applications. Furthermore, the functions that software perform are not usually as simple as a bridge; consequently, software is more difficult to develop and to test. Achieving a lasting solution at the first attempt is expensive and unnecessary in most software developments.

Another major problem with considering software development to be a part of engineering, science, or manufacturing is that this excludes the possibility that software development, or at least some part of it, may be essentially a people-based, creative, and unpredictable activity. If software development is even partly creative, then efforts to manage it in a simplistic or mechanistic fashion may be doomed to failure. The alternative may be ruthlessly to eliminate all potential for creativity, in order to produce a uniform, mass-production approach to software development.

Prototyping can be represented as the antithesis of the traditional and software engineering approaches. There is some truth in this view. Prototyping may also be represented truthfully as an essential component of these approaches. Whatever the conceptual merits and inferential evidence in favour of prototyping, its greatest benefit may be that it offers a more human-oriented alternative to the mechanistic approaches to software development. Prototyping can successfully cope with, and give expression to, the creative view of software development.

Finally, prototyping is about focusing on the needs and demands of the business and the users. It is about people working together continuously, steadily, and harmoniously to put those needs and demands into software in a realistic way. Prototyping is about honesty. It is about being able to make mistakes, to learn from them, and, in the end, to turn them to your advantage. Prototypers do not have to pretend to be perfect and omniscient; prototyping is about making modest improvements and improving them again and again until the optimum degree of quality is reached. Prototyping is about being able to be uncertain and to defer unknowns until it is possible to understand them and to deal with them effectively. Prototyping is an activity that takes place on a human, rather than heroic, scale.

Part Six
Case studies

The two prototyping case studies that follow are fiction. They have been created from a composite of my experience of software development and from my imagination. They are much in the style of cases presented in the well-respected *Harvard Business Review*. I appreciate that this approach is one not often seen in books about computing, but I hope that the reader will appreciate that these are essentially realistic situations.

The fictional approach to case studies has two major advantages over recounting actual cases. First, useful case studies necessarily air problems, mistakes, and personalities. I do not feel that it is right to do this to the companies or people with whom I have worked, even if they would not be easily identifiable. Secondly, fictional case studies can be made more entertaining, instructive, and interesting than real life. Real software developments tend to have few easily identified dramatic moments, nor do they necessarily exhibit all the characteristics I would like to demonstrate in a case study. An author of fiction has opportunities for careful consideration, revision, and improvement that simply do not exist in real life.

Prototyping case I

The First Meeting

'Mr Halykon is free to see you now', said the secretary. She opened the door to John's office. It was chaotic inside; books and papers were piled everywhere.

'Mike, how are you?' cried John, standing. He shook my hand heartily. 'Thanks for coming down to see me. Have a seat, please. Would you like some coffee or tea?'

'No thanks, John. I'm fine', I replied. I took out my notebook and quickly jotted down the details of the visit: person, place, time, and date. 'You have a computer project in mind for me, John?' I asked.

'That's right. Have you ever heard of scripophily?' he asked.

Humour is one of my weaknesses. I swallowed down the witty reply that immediately sprung to mind. 'Er, no, I can't say that I have', I replied smoothly instead. 'What is it?'

'Scripophily is collecting share certificates', he said seriously.

'Oh, you mean apart from collecting them for investment purposes?' I asked.

'Yes, that's right, just like collecting coins. You see, every share certificate is unique. Some of the old issues are really very visually attractive too', John explained. 'Here are some pictures of old certificates', he said, pushing a thick catalogue towards me. It was published by John's company.

I riffled quickly through the book. Most of the certificates were elaborately engraved, like banknotes. A few of them had eye-catching, art deco illustrations. Date, serial number, engraver, condition, and price seemed to be the typical information about the certificates. Some of the catalogue entries had quite a lot of background text about the company that had issued the shares. Prices appeared to be in the £10–100 range; £25 seemed typical. 'So, how do people collect share certificates, John?'

'There is no definite trend, really', replied John. 'Some people collect them by countries, some by industry, others by engraver, and so on. Some people don't specialize at all. There's an awful lot of different types of shares, too, and from a lot of countries. Even ones that don't even exist today. Keeping track of everything is a tremendous job and shares are becoming a main line of my business. I think the computer could be able to help us. I'd like you to look at the job and tell me how much it would cost.'

'Yes, I think that could be possible', I agreed. 'Tell me what it is you want to do first with the computer.'

'Well, for example, a client writes to me and asks for a list of what we've got in North American railway shares, issued between 1890 and 1910. I want a computer to be able to do that for me', he replied.

'That should be possible', I answered.

John looked at me expectantly. 'My neighbour works for a computer company', he said. 'She says that a system expert could do it easily.' He looked extremely pleased with himself for making this suggestion.

'That's an expert system, John', I corrected. 'I'm not really certain that would be the most appropriate way of going about the job. I'll give it consideration, though.' Amateur enthusiasms can be a nuisance, but they also can be valuable 'hooks' to gain interest.

'My neighbour was positive that was the best way', insisted John.

'Yes, it's possible that it would work, but I think it would be premature to get committed to anything like that at this point', I replied. Even as I said that, I knew this job was perfect for a database. I also know that I have a bias for database approaches to almost every application.

'Yes, you could be right,' agreed John, 'but my neighbour was really very convincing about those system experts.'

'Expert systems, John', I corrected again. It was time to change the subject. 'Now, John, does your company use computers for anything else?' I asked.

'Oh, certainly,' he replied brightly, 'My secretary uses a word processor for all the letters. It's one of these PC things.'

'Any other uses?' I asked.

'No, not really,' he replied. 'Nothing that I can think of at the moment . . . Oops! I forgot. She does the accounts on it, too.' He looked even more pleased with himself than before.

I rolled my eyes, mentally. 'Have you got any feel for how much you want to spend, John?' I asked. It is usually a good idea to get past this point before too much time is wasted.

'Well, I had these computer people spend a few days looking at the problem a couple of years ago. They took two whole days just talking to me. They wanted about £10 000 to do the job of writing this software stuff they kept taking about', he said. 'Then, I'd have to buy a computer, too. That was a lot more than I wanted to spend, so I let it drop.'

'You mean this already has been looked at?' I asked with surprise. He hadn't told me that before.

'Oh, yes, it was some government-funded programme or another. Didn't cost me anything', he replied. 'You mean that work could help you?' he asked with surprise.

'No question about it', I replied. 'It could save a couple days of picking your brains, at the least.' I decided that this was the best chance I'd have to let him have some idea of what it might cost. 'But I'm afraid that £10 000 doesn't really go all that far in software development.'

John rose from his desk and walked over to a grey metal filing cabinet. 'Hmmm. Let's see', he said as he opened up a drawer. He leafed through a couple of files and dropped them back in. 'Well, to tell you the truth, Mike, I wasn't so much put off by the price as I didn't have all that much confidence that I'd get what I wanted. They gave me a lot of papers to read and I guess it looked reasonable enough, if you were a computer expert. I scanned over it, but I just couldn't see what the computer was going to do for me. It was just some paper with a lot of boxes and arrows drawn on it. Do you know what I mean?'

'I know exactly what you mean, John', I replied. 'Most people are afraid to admit it, though.'

John looked smug. 'Well, my business is too small to risk that sort of money on something I'm not absolutely sure about', he replied. 'I could buy a year's supply of share certificates to sell for that sort of money. It's a big investment.' He pulled out another file and fingered through it.

'Why are things any different now?' I asked.

John looked up at me with a worried look. 'Times have changed since then, Mike', he said. 'My competitors all seem to be going to computers and increasing their stocks of shares. Everyone's got a lot more customers than they used to. There's too much work for me to do already and I've just got to keep up. I don't want to hire anyone, either. They'd be nothing but trouble. The catalogue alone takes up about half my time. It always seems to be about a year out of date, too. Then, I've got to keep current on what shares are selling for, world wide. I keep on reading in these magazines and newspapers how computers can give businesses competitive edge. Frankly, if I don't get some of that, I'm afraid I'm going to be out of business soon.'

John's face brightened, 'Ah! Here it is. I knew I hadn't thrown it out.' He handed me a report of twenty-odd pages.

I leafed quickly through the report. It looked as though there was a fairly complete analysis and design here. It was just a routine database system, smaller than most applications. 'It says here that the primary objective is to produce catalogues. Is that right?' I asked.

'Well, essentially, yes, I guess', John replied. 'But I think that I might be able to sell the software to recoup my investment.'

'Oh, do you think there's a market for the software?' I asked with interest.

'Oh, there's bound to be', John replied. 'There's just thousands and thousands of collectors out there. I'd guess they'd be glad to spend a couple hundred pounds for a system to keep their collections in order. Then they'd need to buy lots of new information from us to keep up to date.' He rubbed his hands together and smiled broadly.

'Do many of them have computers?' I asked.

'Oh, yes, lots and lots of them must have computers, I'm sure', he replied vaguely.

'Yes, it sounds like a very exciting prospect,' I said. It was the old 'I think the sun is shining, let's set up a lemonade stand' marketing approach. 'Producing software for resale is a pretty different thing from producing software just for your own use, though, John. Which one is more important to you right now?' I asked.

'Oh, I mainly need it to use myself', he said. 'It's just that I keep reading about all these people who make lots and lots of money selling software. I thought that, if your program was good for me, then other people would want it too.'

'That might be true, but you need a lot of investment in cosmetic appearance, slick documentation, support, and extra functions. There are a lot of things to think about', I cautioned. 'I think you should shoot for just doing the immediate application for your own needs.'

I continued leafing through the report. 'What's this about an auction monitor here?' I asked.

'Oh, that's something else I need too', he said. 'Didn't I mention that earlier?'

'Well, you said something about it taking a lot of your time', I said, consulting my notes.

'That's why a program without that ability wouldn't be much use to me', he said breezily. 'I need to be able to enter share prices from auctions and get averages of all types. I use that to set my prices as a dealer. It's so obvious, I thought anyone would know that.'

Good thing I found out about it now, I thought. I said, 'OK. You need to be able to produce catalogues and calculate average auction prices.'

John interrupted, 'I also need to be able to ask the computer questions like, "What's the cheapest Russian gold mining share?" and things like that.'

'Is there anything else you want?' I asked without conscious irony.

'That's just the problem, Mike', said John with a grin. 'I know that I need the program to do those things I mentioned. I can't be sure that's all that I want, though, until I see the computer working. I just don't know enough about computers to be sure. I'm not sure I know how to tell you what I need, even if I knew what it was I needed.'

'Look, John, here's what I'd like to propose', I said. 'I'll spend three days working on your problem, at my normal daily rate. At the end of two days, I'll have a working prototype that I'll demonstrate to you.'

'So fast?' asked John. 'I thought it took a long time to write programs!'

'Once a problem of this type is understood and translated into computing terms, it usually doesn't take more than one or two days to set up a demonstration', I said. 'That is, providing a database management system can do the job. Your previous consultants seem to have done a pretty thorough job of converting your problem into a form I can understand. I'll need the extra day to show you the program and note any problems there may be.'

'You mean my program will be finished then?' he asked happily.

'No, not by a long shot', I answered. His face fell. 'After you use the system, I expect that you'll want to add some items of information. You may want to drop some. You may want more look-up tables and you may want to drop some, too. I'd guess it'll take another two or three days just to get the data formats right.'

'What will happen after that?' John asked cautiously.

'At that point, the most important part of the work will be done. Once you see that, then you need to decide if you want to continue with the project', I said.

'And if I want to continue?' he asked.

'We'll then have to sit down and talk about what computer system you want and which database would be most appropriate', I said.

'You mean I won't be able to run it on my PC?' John asked with concern.

'Yes, you will,' I replied, 'But didn't you say that your secretary uses the PC for letters and accounts? I'd guess she uses it pretty much full time.'

'Yes, she does,' he admitted.

'Then when will you use it?' I asked. 'How will you be able to get enough time on the PC to enter in the large amounts of data about shares and suchlike?'

'I hadn't thought about that', he grumbled.

'We also have to select a suitable database system', I continued.

'Can't we use the one you use?' he asked.

'Yes, but I use a pretty heavy-duty database', I explained. 'You need a top-of-the-line PC to run it and that's expensive to buy. On the other hand, it's a database that will run on almost every computer sold, from PC to mainframe, and it won't run out of steam if the database gets big. No matter what, you'll need to make some investment in new hardware and software.'

'I didn't think it would be all this complicated', he said unhappily. 'I mean it's not like going to the store and just getting a PC.'

'Oh, even that's not the end of it yet, John', I continued. 'Off the top of my head, I'd guess the catalogue program will take about five days work. You'll also want to be able to generate maybe half a dozen analysis reports from your database. Typically, it takes about a day to program a report. A lot of that depends on how fancy you want the reports to look, though.'

'Are you trying to put me off this or something, Mike?' he asked with exasperation.

'No, I'm not John,' I said, 'I'm just trying to give you a realistic idea of what's involved. I'd guess it will take a minimum of twenty days work after the first phase. I'll have a lot better idea after I do the prototype. A lot of the time needed will depend on your involvement: how carefully you look at what I show you, how easily satisfied you are, and suchlike.'

John looked uncomfortable. 'Well, of course, I'll put in as much time as it needs. I'll certainly know what I want if I see it. I'll be able to tell you what I don't like.'

'I'm sure you will', I said. 'The good news, John, is that you'll be able to see and try what you're getting as we go along. After the essential parts are done, you can stop if it's getting too expensive. At least you'll have something that works and that you can be sure you like.'

'I think I can see the advantage of what you're talking about, Mike', he mused. His face still looked worried. 'Those other fellows wanted me to commit to the full £10 000 after just seeing their report.' He thought for a few seconds and toyed with his pen. Finally, his face brightened. 'OK, it makes sense,' he said, 'Let's go for the first three days and then let's take it as it goes from there.'

The Second Meeting

'Thanks for coming here to see the demonstration, John', I said. I walked over and we shook hands.

'It's a pleasure, Mike.' he said, 'Especially if I'll really be able to see this program working right now. The drive over here was nice too.'

'Well,' I said, 'I more or less followed the work that was laid out by your previous consultants. We'll see how well they did.' I switched on the PC. 'How about some coffee?'

'Ummm, that would be lovely. White with sugar', he replied. He sat down and looked eagerly at the computer. I fixed and brought him a cup of coffee.

'Right,' I said, 'Let's get started then.' I jotted down the date and time in my notebook. I typed in the start-up command and the first entry screen came up.

'Oh, gosh!' exclaimed John happily, 'That's a screen to describe share issues!' He looked carefully at it. 'What's that serial number thingy?' he asked.

'The computer generates that automatically, so that each issue can be identified uniquely', I replied.

'You mean I don't have to give the numbers myself?' he asked.

'That's right', I replied. 'You can then use that number to refer to the issues, instead of the name.'

'Hmmm,' he replied, 'I'm not sure that's very useful. Does it have to be there?'

'No. I can take it off, if you decide you don't want it', I said. 'I think you'll find it useful, though.' I set up a search and retrieved a record.

His face lit up. 'You've got a share there! That's amazing! Wonderful!' he cried. 'It's one of my certificates. How on earth did you do that?'

'Oh, I just used one of your old catalogues', I replied, pleased by his pleasure. 'I needed to enter some data to see if the data layout would work with your catalogue. In fact, I had a problem understanding some of the data structure so I had to guess.'

John looked concerned. 'Is that serious?' he asked. 'These data structure things?'

'I won't know until you've had a look at the rest', I replied. I flicked through a dozen records until the 'last record' message came up.

'What's the matter?' he asked. 'Is this the problem you were talking about?'

'No, no,' I laughed. 'That's just the end of the data. I only entered a dozen issues.'

John looked relieved. 'Whew. I thought there was something wrong.' He peered at the last record and pointed to the date-of-issue field. 'Could that be moved after the name of the issue', he asked.

'Oh yes,' I confirmed, 'Moving the fields around is no problem. It takes about ten minutes per field.' I made a note in my book. 'Don't worry about that sort of thing now. All we want to do now is to make sure that all the data you need are here.'

'Well, it all looks just fine to me, Mike', he said briskly. 'Is this all?' he asked. He started to get up. I could see he was getting bored already.

'Oh, no,' I replied, 'There's a lot more yet, John.' I knew he hadn't really looked at this screen yet. I flicked to the next screen anyway. 'Here's a description of an issue. I wasn't sure whether it belonged to a share or to an issue.'

'I'm not sure what you mean', replied John. 'You see, a company might have any number of share issues during its life. It's the share you need to describe.'

'Shouldn't that mean that we should have a company description too?' I asked.

'Oh yes, you need to know all about companies', he replied brightly. 'Wasn't that in the report?'

'Not as far as I could see', I replied with that slightly sinking feeling. I knew that these points would mean a major design change to the system.

'Is that a problem?' asked John. He looked at the screen carefully. 'I think this description thing is pretty good, but it really should be part of the share description. You see,' he explained, 'Each issue can have different types of shares, such as founder certificates and bearer bonds. Usually, the different types of shares look a bit different and are a different colour. It makes a difference to scarcity and price, you see. I thought that everyone knew that.'

I could see by now that the initial design and my understanding had been faulty. The design was more or less 'upside-down'. I decided to demonstrate the rest of the system without mentioning structural problems any more. I showed John how to use the software. I got him to type in some entries from his catalogue. There were the usual requests to lengthen fields, add a few fields, drop some fields, and change the position of everything. There was nothing that, in total, probably couldn't be handled in a good day's work. Well, make that three days. That wasn't counting, of course, the structural problems.

'Well, John,' I said, 'How do you like what you've seen.'

'Oh, it's very good, Mike', he replied enthusiastically. 'I think it's just about what I want, except for the few little things I've mentioned. How long do you think it will take to get it ready for me to use? Can I take it back with me?'

'Well, there's a problem with the structure of the software, as implemented from the report', I said.

His eyebrows shot up. 'What does that mean?' he asked.

'It means maybe an extra day of work to fix those problems, a day to make the other changes you've asked for today and then another presentation', I said.

John pursed his lips, 'Another three days. How much after that?'

I referred to my notebook. 'Well, the first phase looks like taking eight, instead of five days. It still should be about the same, overall, as I indicated in our first meeting. Maybe 20–25 days in all. We shouldn't have any more major problems if we get the structure right at the first.'

John looked at the screen. 'How about putting in two more days work? Then we'll decide where we want to go from there', he proposed.

I knew I was being squeezed. Maybe I shouldn't have jumped to implementation on the basis of the old analysis documentation. I decided to give him a free day or two. I said, 'Tell you what, John. It's going to need three days. You pay for two and I'll throw in one day free, providing you come here again for the next demonstration.'

'OK,' he agreed happily, 'Let's do that.'

The Third Meeting

'John,' I said confidently, 'I think you're really going to like what you see today.' The system was really slick now.

He rubbed his hands together. 'I certainly hope so,' he said happily, 'I've been thinking a lot about this.'

'Good', I replied. 'I've spent a bit more time than we agreed. I put in the auction part and I even got it in to handle foreign currencies.' Actually, I'd been carried away with enthusiasm and spent an extra three days. I was sure my extra work wouldn't be wasted. I knew an awful lot more about share certificates now, probably as much as John did in some ways. I knew too that he was going to like what he saw. 'Great. That does sound exactly what I need', said John.

'What I'd like for you to do first, John, is to sit down and put in a dozen catalogue entries for me', I said. I pushed a thin manual toward him. 'This should tell you everything you need to know to run the system. If you have any trouble, I'll just be in the next room. Shout if you need me.' I thought that this would force him to really get to grips with the system. I'd also spent a day extra preparing the documentation.

I hadn't sat down for five minutes before there was a plaintive bleat from John. 'Mike! How do you turn this blasted computer thing on?'

I went in and turned the PC on for him. I made a note to put that into the documentation. It was a mistake to assume any level of knowledge. I should know that by now. I sat next to him while he started up the PC. He followed the instructions and soon got the screens running. I went back to my office. About half an hour later I poked my head in. 'How's it going?' I asked.

John looked up at me with a disappointed expression. 'It takes so long to enter in things', he complained. 'I'm only on my second one. There's a problem with some of the certicate classifications too. There's a lot of things that just don't fit.'

'Practice will speed up your entry time', I said. 'I timed myself and it only took me five minutes for each entry. I put in the classifications you had in the report. Those can be changed for you. Don't worry about that, it's just data. How does it look otherwise?' I asked.

'It looks fine to me, so far', he said. 'Let me put in a few more and I'll have a better idea. I guess I'll be able to use those classifications. They're the ones I use now, anyway. I just expected that the computer would give me better ones than that.'

'The computer is only as good as the information it gets, John', I reminded him as I went back to my office. I knew he didn't really believe that, though.

About an hour later, John called jubilantly, 'Mike! I'm done.'

I went in and sat down next to him. 'Let's see what you've done', I said. I flicked through the database. It looked all right to me, except for a tendency to enter a lot of trivial remarks. 'That looks good. Did you find anything that should have been there and wasn't?' I asked.

'No, not really,' he said reflectively, 'I think you could add more room for remarks, if it wouldn't be too much trouble. I liked the auction part a lot. That looks just right.' I made a note to extend the remarks fields. 'Mike, do you think this program would be good enough to sell?' he asked suddenly.

'Well, John, we spoke about that at our first meeting. I think it would take a lot of work to get it the way people expect software to be when they buy it.' I had a nasty suspicion I knew what was coming up. 'You'd need it to be full of data before anyone would buy it, too.'

'Yes, but it works perfectly well the way it is here right now', he protested. 'I like it. I'd pay £500 for it without giving it a thought,' he said, 'so why can't it be sold?'

'It's only a prototype,' I explained. 'Your customers would have to spend five times as much on the database software and on hardware as they would on your software. You couldn't make money at anything near the price you mentioned unless you had hundreds of customers.' This was the problem with using this database management system. It did a good job and was suitable for delivering minicomputer and mainframe solutions. It was too expensive for mass-market PC software, though. 'What's the pressure to sell the software right away?' I asked.

He looked sheepishly at me. 'Well, things have changed in the business since the last time we spoke', he explained. 'I've hired an assistant, my niece actually, to take over that part of the business. She's just got an MBA. I'm not really sure it's cheaper to use a computer than it is to pay her to do it. Anyway, she says she knows something about computers from school.'

I gave it a last try. 'But, John, the computer will allow you to make all different sorts of catalogues and price lists. It'll take a fraction of the time it does manually and be more accurate. As long as you keep up the auction lists, you'll have the best possible information to research prices.'

'Yes, I know all that, Mike', he said. 'But I really don't think it'll be worth keeping all that information up to date, unless I can also sell it to collectors or other dealers. Selling the program would allow me to do that. Besides, now that I've got a new employee, I don't really think I can afford the development, just for internal use, right at this moment.'

'But you remember I told you that developing the software for external sale would cost a lot more?' I asked.

'Yes, but I might be able to get some government grants or something like that', he said vaguely. 'My neighbour says her company gets them all the time. They get lots of money, too. She says they might be willing to help me with it, using these expert thingies.'

'Well, look, John,' I said with relief, 'Why don't you do this? Find some potential customers and I'll demonstrate this prototype to them. If you find the market out there for the software, then we can work up a plan to pre-sell it and convert the prototype into a real product.'

He looked relieved. 'That sounds like a great idea, Mike', he said. 'I'll get ads into all the collectors' journals right away and see what the response is. I'll give you a call as soon as something looks promising.'

I'm still waiting for John's call. At least he paid his bill.

Discussion

What a disappointment! Or was it? On the face of it, prototyping seemed to lose the narrator a contract. With an analytical approach, he might have revised the earlier specifications and been able to talk John into a development contract. On the other hand, the narrator might have wasted as much time preparing a detailed proposal and still had no contract. At least with the prototype, the narrator was paid for five days work.

Had the narrator been able to convince John to go ahead, he almost certainly would have faced trouble. John did not have a clear idea of what he wanted or even if he wanted anything at all. His business changed radically during the short prototyping period. There is doubt about how much time and money he really would have been prepared to spend. Had John gone ahead with the development, it is possible that he would have found reasons why the software was unsatisfactory and avoided payment.

The narrator made a serious mistake in seizing uncritically on the earlier consultants' work. He raced off to do the first prototype without gaining any real understanding of the subject. John might have led him to the wrong design too, but half an hour of discussion might have saved some work. The narrator's enthusiasm was commendable, but prototyping still requires getting a grip on the subject matter before starting. A more astute client might have insisted on the narrator's footing the bill for the rework or have used the error as an excuse to drop the project without paying for it.

Another tactical mistake was that the narrator put more work into the prototype than was necessary. Again, his enthusiasm led him astray. He put in the auction and currency functions at his own expense, even though John did not demand them during the second meeting. The narrator got a pat on the back from John, but it made no difference to the outcome to the contract.

In this case, prototyping was not only useful for arriving at an apparently satisfactory technical solution, it also provided a prototype business experience of working with the client. As so often happens, business with John was not as good as the narrator had hoped it would be. The good thing was that the narrator found that out with partial compensation and with only a modest amount of wasted effort. The gradual approach of prototyping allowed the development to be scrapped before either party had committed too much to it.

Prototyping case II

Part 1

'Mr Halykon is free to see you now', said the secretary. She opened the door to John's office. It was bigger and more luxurious, but it was still chaotic inside. Books and papers were piled everywhere.

'Well, Mike, it's been a long time. How are you?' cried John, standing. He shook my hand heartily. 'I've never forgotten that work you did for me when Collectibles was just a one-man band. You did a very good job and saved me money when I needed it most. I learned a lot from that.'

'Me too, John', I replied honestly.

'Well, how about some coffee or tea?' he boomed.

'No thanks, John. I've just had some', I said. I took out my notebook and took down the details of the visit. 'How can I help you this time?' I asked.

'Well, Mike,' he said, 'The Collectibles Group has come a long way since the last time we met. It's now the national market leader in ephemera and we're beginning to make the big boys sweat a bit in the auctions everywhere. We've diversified and our operations are international. We've got about a 170 staff and six offices, world-wide.'

I smiled. 'I've been keeping track of what you've been doing since your flotation. I went for a thousand myself', I admitted.

John beamed with pleasure. 'Oh, well done! Perhaps I should call you "sir", in that case.' We both laughed. 'Anyway, Mike, I think Collectibles has problems with its computers again. Nothing seems to get done any more and I need better information than I'm getting. A lot better information, I can tell you.'

I was interested, of course. 'Well, tell me about your present computer operations, John.'

'Do you remember Alice, Mike?' he asked.

I made a wild guess. 'Is she your niece?' I asked?

'That's right', he said. 'My first real employee. She took over shares from me and made a very good thing out of it too. She added toys about a year later and really made them go. Well, you know, she had a good background in computers from her MBA. So when we got Megalith Computing in to install our computers, it was natural for her to take charge of that side of the business too.'

'Megalith is a good outfit for accounting systems', I replied stiffly. I was still a bit irritated that he hadn't called me in for that one.

'Yes, there've certainly been no problems with the bookkeeping stuff, all right', said John. 'The trouble is, our business is pretty specialized, so we needed some special programs. Megalith haven't got a clue about that. So, Alice hired this fellow called Bob Clark. Well, Bob took over the computer and did some really good work for us. For a few years, an awful lot got done and it got done fast. He made that computer really jump through the hoop. The computing department grew to a half dozen people. Unfortunately, Bob moved on.'

'That's only to be expected in the computer business', I said.

'So I've found out', growled John. 'Those people just don't seem to have any loyalty to the company at all. You know, I offered him a 5 per cent pay rise and that fellow still went. Anyway, Alice hired some more people and took direct control again. Things just don't seem to be moving any more though. All my managers have been complaining for ages. They say things are much worse than they were when Bob was here. Alice says that the computer systems are just fine, but that the users are all morons.'

'Computing operations often run out of steam after a good start', I commented tactfully.

'Well, this one certainly seems to have', agreed John. 'To make matters worse, most of the other offices have computers. They've all gone out and each one's done something different, it seems. It's beginning to look like a real mess to me, Mike. Last week, my finance director showed me figures proving that we're spending at least 15 per cent of our gross income on computers!'

'In my experience, that's not an unusual amount, John', I said.

'That may be, but Collectibles is still much too small to put that kind of money into something that's not working', said John. He looked miserable for a moment. 'Besides, I'm just not getting the information I need to run the business. I'm getting out of touch. It's all the computer's fault too.'

'It's probably not as bad as you think, John', I said comfortingly. It was probably worse, I thought.

'Look, I was really impressed with the work you did for me before, Mike. You know how to make computers work', he said. 'Tell me what you think I ought to do to get things moving again.'

I smiled at him. He should have been impressed, I did a fantastic bit of work for him before. 'You'll have to be willing to spend some money on the problem, first of all', I said. Now we were going to hear the pips squeak, I thought with glee.

'Well, that's why you're here today, Mike', he said expansively. 'We've just got to get our computers working for us again. Tell me what you want to do.'

I thought for a moment. 'OK. First thing is for me to go in and do a survey of your total computer operations, world-wide. I'll look at your hardware, software, and people. Talk to everyone involved, including your users.' John nodded in agreement. 'I'll look where things are working and where they're not working. Then I'll give you a status report and solid recommendations as to what I think you should do.'

'Yes,' said John, 'That all sounds very sensible. How much will it cost?'

I thought of a figure that might make him uncomfortable and doubled it. I doubled it again. I let him have it.

'Good grief!' he exploded. 'You can't possibly be serious!'

'Plus expenses,' I added quickly. I sat back and waited.

John hemmed and hawed and fiddled with his pen. I saw him quickly calculate how much he might be losing from his computer operation. 'Oh, all right', he said grumpily. 'Not expenses, though. When can you start?'

Part 2

I could see that the management committee's interest was high, so I decided to wrap up the presentation while I was still ahead. 'So, in summary, I have found that the headquarters computing operation is both competent and professional. Its maintenance of existing software, written in RPG II, is as good as can be expected for the level of technology.' Alice looked very satisfied with herself. She'd made sure that computing's best foot had been put forward during the survey. You could see her staff shaking in their boots in case they slipped and told me the truth.

I smiled at Alice and resumed. 'It seems to be agreed, however, that there appears to be a serious quantity problem in the production of new software.'

'He's right there', put in Alice quickly. 'That's because computing doesn't have enough staff or a big enough budget.'

I let the comment pass and pressed on, 'The introduction of a fourth-generation language, now in progress, should result in more rapid generation of end user software.' Alice nodded in agreement.

'There is, however, a serious problem in the relations between the computing staff and the users. I believe this is key to the quantity problem with software', I said.

Alice took this as criticism. 'That's because the users don't know anything', she interjected. 'They don't even know how their own business works. They want the moon, but they don't know how they want it. If they make up their minds one day, they change them the next. If,' she rasped, 'They have any minds at all.' This got a little laugh around the table, except from Albert, the head of administration.

Albert snapped, 'Well, it's just not the job of other people to be computer experts! That's your job, Alice. We know our jobs and don't ask your computer department to do them. A lot of people here are worried about losing their jobs to the computer, too. Everyone knows that your computer staff get paid a whole lot more than anyone else does. Why don't they just start earning it for a change, instead of pushing people around and wasting time and money?'

'It's impossible to keep computer staff if we don't pay them competitive salaries', stated Alice condescendingly. 'We're understaffed as it is!'

'They don't stay anyway!' retorted Albert. 'They just use us as the bottom rung of a career ladder. They've got no loyalty to anyone but themselves.'

'Ah, Alice, Albert,' I interrupted gently, 'Do you think I could finish my report, please? Then we can open the floor for discussion.' Alice stuck her nose up in the air and crossed her arms. Albert glowered at his desk. Fred, the finance director, smiled. John looked worried.

I continued, 'Alice has recently proposed that Collectibles makes a major investment in computer-aided software engineering to overcome its problems in software development quality.'

John interrupted. 'That's right', he said brightly. 'My neighbour works for this new computer start-up company. She told me that this engineering software stuff can improve productivity a whole lot. They have this CASE thingy that's just absolutely amazing, she says. She says its the way to go, for sure.'

'Well, John,' I replied, 'Computer-aided software engineering, CASE, has been developed mainly for software design in the defence and aerospace industry. I have serious doubts about its immediate value to a company the size of Collectibles, doing the type of computing Collectibles does. Your company's really pretty small for that level of investment.' John shot a worried glance at Alice.

'Anyway,' I concluded, 'I think your problem isn't really about bad design or implementation of software. I think it's mostly about the problems of communications between your users and your computer staff. In fact, I think CASE not only won't help your communication problems, I think it could make it a lot worse.'

'Now that's absolutely preposterous!' cried Alice. 'Why, I could get ten experts in here tomorrow who would give exactly the opposite view.'

'Yes, you could', I replied. 'And every one of those experts would be salespeople of one form or another. Their evidence would be stories about companies a hundred times the size of yours, doing applications a hundred times the size of yours.'

'The principles are just the same', asserted Alice. 'It's just a matter of scale.'

'That isn't proven', I said. 'More seriously, if you had these software engineers talk to your users, I'm sure none of your users would have the faintest idea what they were talking about.'

Alice looked puzzled. 'I don't understand what you mean.'

'How many of your users understand data flow diagrams or entity relationship modelling?' I asked.

'Well, none of them, of course!' she snapped. 'They don't know anything about computers. I already told you that. They couldn't blow their noses on computer paper!'

'What makes you think they're going to understand highly technical output from CASE, then?' I asked.

'Well, it's all diagrams', Alice replied, a little hesitant for the first time. 'The users look at these pictures and understand what's going on. They can browse through the diagrams and change them easily. There's lots of different types of diagrams for them to see. They don't have to use data flow diagrams if they don't know how to use those. Lots of different methodologies are supported.'

'If you haven't had much luck explaining your systems to users in English,' no doubt very plain English, I thought, 'Then how do you think you're going to get them to learn highly technical software engineering techniques?' I asked.

Alice looked at her watch. 'Look, I really have other things I must do', she said frostily. 'Why don't you just get on with your proposal?'

'Thank you', I said drily. 'As I said, you have just adopted a fourth-generation language. This change is an excellent opportunity for the computer operation to evaluate a different approach toward software development: prototyping.' Alice pulled a wry face. 'In many ways, prototyping is the opposite of the analytical approach practised by Collectibles at present.'

Alice jumped at this. 'You can say that again! We do things right in my outfit!' she cried. 'Feasibility, analysis, customer sign-off, development, testing, delivery. Are you trying to say this is wrong?'

'For Collectibles, yes', I said flatly.

Alice fell back in her chair in mock amazement. She looked at John in appeal. 'John, this is just crazy. I never heard such a thing in my life. This guy is talking through his hat.' John just looked very worried.

'Alice,' I asked, 'Do you feel that your software meets the needs of your users?'

'Of course it does', she snapped. 'I don't do any developments, buster, until that manager signs on the dotted line. They don't get anything either until that software meets the specification that they signed.'

'And what kind of specification do they sign?' I asked.

'You know very well what kind of specification they sign', she growled. 'You took copies of every one we had.'

'Exactly', I said. 'I looked carefully at them too. Each one was a detailed and intricate software design, down to module specification level. They are highly technical documents.'

'There's no other way you can do a useful spec', she said defensively; then more agressively, 'Those specs were signed off! Every one of them! I can show you. We have programmed every system exactly to specification too! They got exactly what they signed for!'

I turned to Albert. 'Albert, you've signed off three specifications in two years. Did you get the software you wanted.'

Albert's eyes blazed. 'I don't know if I got the software I wanted or not, whatever that is. But, I'll tell you what, I sure didn't get what I expected! And it was late, too!'

'Well, Albert, if that's true,' demanded Alice, 'Why did you sign off the specs, then?'

'I talked to your people and they explained what they were going to do. It sounded reasonable when they said it', Albert replied. 'You don't expect me to read all that gobbledegook they throw around? I'm not a computer expert!' He looked disgusted. 'You don't have to be an expert, though, to see that what they gave us won't do what we need! Most of it's garbage! We had to pay for it, too, but we can't use it. My people never even used that crazy ordering system you tried to push down their throats.'

The finance director, Fred, spoke for the first time. 'We didn't seem to have all these problems when Bob was here, Alice', he said softly.

'Bob! Huh!' huffed Alice. 'He was just a jumped-up clerk who owned a home computer. He was a total amateur! He only did the easy jobs anyway. His documentation was rubbish and he did things in the stupidest way. We've had to rewrite almost everything he did to meet our internal standards. No wonder we've got maintenance problems now.'

'At least Bob gave us what we wanted', retorted Albert. 'He did it fast and he kept at it until we got what we wanted. We couldn't care less about your internal standards. All we want is things that work.'

'That's because you don't understand anything about computers!' shouted Alice. 'It's all got to work together!'

'But Alice,' said Fred in an even tone, 'We don't really want to know anything about computers. That's your job. We just want them to do what we need them to do, when we need them, and for what we can afford to pay.'

Alice turned on John. 'I've had enough of this, John', she said. 'I've got another meeting and I'm going to it, right now.' She glared at the rest of us. 'I've read his proposal. He proposes to prototype the new order system, using the new fourth-generation language that I selected.'

I nodded. 'That's right', I said.

'Well, I'm too busy to do that development this year, anyway', she snapped. 'If the rest of you agree to this crazy project, then he can have Harry for three months to do it his way. As long as he doesn't get in the way of my department. I've already done a feasibility study and an outline of the business functions for the new ordering system. That's my contribution. You can pay for him,' she pointed at me, 'Out of your budgets. Now, if you'll excuse me, I'll get on back to work', she said, smiling thinly. She stood up and barged out of the room.

John coughed. 'I, er, take it the motion is carried?' he asked. Those remaining nodded their assent.

Part 3

'Good morning, Mrs Edgely', I said, smiling. Harry mumbled an unintelligible noise at her and found something interesting to look at out of the window.

'Oh, please call me Sue', she said. 'All my friends do.'

'Well, Sue, we're here to talk to you about the new computer program for orders', I said. 'Albert Rumpleton says that you're the person who knows the most about ordering.'

'Well, I don't know about that', she said warily. 'I mean, I do a lot of the ordering, but I don't know how much I'll be able to help you with computers. I'm not technical, you see.'

The phone rang and Sue snatched it up. It was a customer with a query about an order. I took the opportunity to take notes about what she was doing. She looked nervously at me as I did. No sooner had the first call finished than a second one came in. 'You'll have to excuse me', she said, flustered. 'I've just had an urgent call from a customer in Germany, I have to run over to the shipping department.' She looked around. 'I tell you what. Why don't you just talk to Ellen for now?' She dashed off down the corridor.

We got up and moved across the room. 'Good morning, Ellen', I said. Harry grunted something.

'Oh,' Ellen said sharply, 'It's the computer people, is it? Are you new? They've got so many people, it's hard to keep track of them all. Not like us, there's only three of us here in ordering.' She looked spitefully at Harry. Harry looked as though he wanted to evaporate. I guessed he'd probably need an extra two hours of video games tonight to recover from the real world.

'Ah, I'm a consultant working just on this project', I said. Being nice only goes so far with some people. It looked necessary to pull rank a bit. 'I'm working directly for Mr Halykon on this project. He's taking a personal interest in it.'

She obviously knew who he was. 'Oh, well then,' she said with a friendly smile to me, 'That's different. How can I be of help to you?'

'I'd like you to show me what you do in your work', I replied. 'I hope you don't mind if I take notes. It helps me keep things straight later on.'

'Of course not,' she replied. 'Now the first thing we do when we get an order is this.' She pulled out a set of forms.

'Oh, do you think I could have a full set of those forms?' I asked. Forms are one of the best way of getting started with a prototype.

'Of course you can', she said, warming up. 'I helped design some of these, you know.'

Now she's hooked, I thought. Most people love to talk about how they do their jobs, once they get started. Ellen certainly did. In an hour, I must have taken 20 pages of dense notes and scribbled all over the forms too. Harry spent most of his time looking out of the window and probing his nose.

'And so that's how we handle the order when it comes in', she said breathlessly. 'Now here's what we do once we have the order', she started.

'Whoa, Ellen, whoa!' I laughed. 'That's about all I can soak up in one sitting.' I stretched my writing hand and flexed it.

'Well, it is an awful lot to do,' she said happily, 'Isn't it? I mean we're just busy morning until night, every day. We've got so much to do. That's just with the paperwork. We don't really have time even to look at all the problems we hear about.'

Here was an opportunity to lay in a bit of propaganda for the new system. 'Well, you know, Ellen, the computer will help you an awful lot with the routine sort of paperwork', I said. 'You'll find it a lot easier to track orders. You'll have more time to handle problem orders. Besides, you'll be getting computer experience. That's got to be pretty valuable to anyone these days.'

'Yes, that would be just lovely', she said uncertainly. She looked around carefully and asked in a low voice, 'Do you think they'll need as many of us here after the computer comes in?'

'In my experience, Ellen,' I said, 'The computer won't put people out of their jobs in a company this size. If all goes well, it may mean that the company won't have to hire more people as its business grows. It probably won't even take less time for you to fill out an order on the computer. It should save time on preparing reports and searching for things, though. A lot of your work should shift to doing things you probably need to to, but just don't have time.'

'Oh, yes,' she said, nodding her head, 'There's plenty of those kind of jobs. Why just last week, Mr Rumpleton . . .'

I interrupted smoothly. 'Now, what we'd like to do now, Ellen, is actually to produce an order form on the computer and show it to you. That way we can see if we've missed anything today.'

'Oh goody,' she said eagerly, 'Let me see it now.' Harry rolled his eyes and looked disgusted. Ellen scowled at him.

I laughed. 'No, Ellen, we'll have to go away for a few days and work on it. Then we'll be back to show it to you.'

Part 4

'Harry,' I snapped, 'What's the matter with you?'

'What do you mean?' he replied sullenly.

'Don't you want to work on this project?' I asked.

'Yeah, I guess so', he said. 'It's a change from doing maintenance on mouldy old ratpurge programs.'

'Ratpurge?' I asked.

'RPG', he replied haughtily. 'I thought everybody knew that.'

'Well, if you want to work with me, you're going to have to change some of your attitudes', I snapped. 'The way you act with the users isn't acceptable. They have information to give you. They have ideas. They want to be heard. You didn't listen. You weren't even polite.'

'Yeah?' he said sceptically, 'Did you hear what she said when you said hello to her? That wasn't exactly polite either. Besides, what do users know about anything?'

'There's often a lot of bad feeling towards computer people', I said. 'It sort of goes with the job. If you can't handle it, then you probably shouldn't be dealing with users.'

'Look,' he protested, 'I'm supposed to be a computer programmer, not a salesman. You don't have to soft soap computers all the time. You just have to know what you're doing. Computers don't slag you off when some little thing goes wrong with the weather.'

'Well, Harry, if you don't sell your developments to users, you won't get many chances to program', I replied. 'I know there's been a lot of friction here, but this is a chance to change that.'

Harry looked thoughtful. 'What's in it for me?' he asked.

'Write software that people really need. More fun, less hassle. More responsibility and less bureaucracy for you', I suggested.

'How less bureaucracy?' he asked with sudden interest.

'Instead of someone else writing a spec and then you programming to it, we do almost the reverse', I explained.

'What? You mean I write the program first and then someone else writes the spec?' he asked in disbelief. 'That's not the way we work around here. Alice will bust her spats.'

'I suppose all your programs work first time?' I countered.

He grinned sheepishly. 'Not quite. What usually happens is the delivered program isn't right because the spec isn't right. Alice would blow her stack if she knew that. So we deliver it to the users. Frank, the software manager, tells Alice that the stuff has been delivered to spec and that it's now in maintenance. Under maintenance, we just hack it around until we more or less fix what's wrong or missing. So, I guess maybe we just about do what you suggest most of the time anyway. Alice and Frank will never buy it, though', he added.

'Well, prototyping takes changes in management attitude too', I said.

'That wouldn't be such a bad thing', said Harry.

'All right, then,' I asked, 'Are you with me?'

'Yeah, OK,' he said with a grin, 'Why not? I'll give it a whirl. It can't be any worse than what we're doing now. Besides, it might be interesting to get out of the back room for a while.'

Part 5

'Oooh,' said Ellen, 'Just look at that! It's our order form! How ever did you do that, Harry?'

'Oh, that's pretty easy', he said confidently. 'I just used your forms as an example. It's easy when you have such good material to work from.' He smiled shyly at Ellen and she smiled back.

'I don't like the colours you've used', complained Sue. 'They're going to hurt our eyes.'

'They don't hurt my eyes, Sue', mumbled Harry.

'Well, you won't have to sit in front of that computer, hour after hour, day after day!' snapped Sue.

'I sit all day in front of something like this and it's OK for me', said Harry defensively.

'They look all right to me, Sue', said Ellen. 'Harry asked me what colours I wanted.'

'Oh, I see', said Sue sulkily. 'Come on then, get on with it then, we've got a lot of work to do today. Big batch of orders in from Germany this morning. Those might just help pay for some of your salary', she sneered.

'This will just take the hour which was agreed we'd spend', insisted Harry, gritting his teeth. He demonstrated the software for a few minutes. A few minor points of style were raised and Harry promised to change them.

Harry quickly show Ellen how to use the program. 'Hey,' he said with surprise, 'You're catching on to this really quick.'

Ellen flushed happily. 'It's not all that hard', she said. 'Once you get used to it.' She took out some orders and started typing them in. 'This is great, Harry, but where do we put our initials when we've finished?' she asked.

'Oh,' asked Harry, 'Is that on the form?'

'No, we write it on the back,' replied Ellen. 'But I did tell you. I think I did, anyway.'

'Well, no matter', said Harry easily. 'That won't take much time to put in. How is it otherwise?'

'The order date comes up as today. Can we change it?' asked Ellen.

'You just type over it if it's not today', explained Harry.

'I've tried, but it won't work', said Ellen with concern. 'What have I done wrong?'

'See, I told you! I told you!' cried Sue triumphantly. 'It doesn't work!'

'It does so work', said Harry with irritation. 'I must have forgotten to allow that field to be changed. It'll just take a minute to fix. It's just a prototype. It's not supposed to work.'

'Oh, yeah, sure!' rasped Sue. 'I've heard that from you people before. Everything's easy, except getting things working on time!'

Harry's face set with determination. 'Please, Ellen, let me sit there for a minute', he said. Harry made both changes in less than five minutes. The women watched him work. 'There.' he said triumphantly, 'I've fixed them! Try it again, please.'

Ellen sat down and tried it. 'Oh, Harry,' Ellen said, 'That's just wonderful. You must be really smart to know how to do all that.' Harry blushed and smiled shyly.

'All right, lovebirds, cool it', interrupted Sue sourly. 'I'm getting pretty tired of looking at all this computer stuff. I guess it looks good enough for me, if you put in what we've talked about. When do you think you're going to have this stupid program ready for us to use, wonder boy?'

Part 6

I knocked and stuck my head through Alice's office door. 'I thought that you'd be interested in the progress of the prototyping experiment', I said.

'Oh, Harry's been keeping me pretty much up to date on it', she said neutrally. She waved for me to sit across from her desk. I knew that Harry didn't much look forward to his weekly interrogations by Alice.

'Good', I said. 'Then you know that the order system seems to be going well. The first part is now in daily use. We've finished this phase of the development in a month. Enhancement requests have bottomed out, at least for now.'

'You've done only up to capturing orders and generating invoices', she reminded me.

'Plus management reports', I added.

'OK,' she shrugged. 'So it's gone well. So what?'

'Do you accept that prototyping might be a valid approach to software development?' I asked.

Alice's face set. 'As a manager, I just can't accept any unstructured approach which says, "Just let people run hog wild with the company's time and money" ', she said.

'Alice, that isn't what prototyping is about at all', I said patiently. 'It's about reducing or replacing the traditional analysis and development approach with an evolutionary approach which directly involves the users.

You can make prototyping as structured and disciplined as you want.'

'If I use prototyping, then how am I supposed to plan and estimate the resources a development's going to need?' she asked.

'Are you using a formal estimation method for software development now?' I asked.

'No,' she admitted, 'Our company's too small for that sort of thing. It takes a couple of people just to maintain the database and methodologies. The software alone costs thousands to buy.'

'Then how do you estimate what a project is going to need?' I asked.

'We go in, spend a day or so looking at the problem and make an estimate, based on our experience', she replied.

'In prototyping, you'd do the same thing', I said. 'There's no implication that you don't have to think carefully about what you're doing or ignore planning when you're prototyping.'

'Yes, but you might have to do the development a couple of times with prototyping', she said quickly. 'Then your estimate would be totally off. You might end up working on it forever. How do you know when to stop.'

'Most people get tired after a few cycles. You didn't hear anyone wanting another go at the prototype, did you?'

'No,' she admitted, 'But what if someone just won't stop?'

'Prototyping needs strong, able management to say that development has gone on long enough', I said. I looked confidently at Alice. Flattery may not be noble, but it can be highly effective at times.

Alice lifted her chin confidently. 'Oh, yes, I can provide that, all right', she agreed.

'Besides, doesn't more software end up being worked on for its entire lifetime, anyway?' I asked.

'What do you mean by that?' she countered suspiciously.

'Aren't you spending at least three-quarters of your resources on maintenance?' I asked.

'Possibly half', admitted Alice. 'But most of that's enhancement, not bug fixing. At least, once the software shakes down after delivery.'

'Demands for enhancement are really a sort of compliment, you know. If software's any good, people will want it to keep up with changes in the business and to do more things, won't they?' I asked. 'Software must evolve with the business.'

Alice nodded. 'So you're saying that prototyping may shift some of the development effort up front, but that it will reduce maintenance?'

'I'm not really saying quite that, although it's true', I replied. 'What I'm saying is that most software development is evolutionary anyway, even with traditional approaches. Given that, we might as well extend the evolutionary aspects forward and manage it properly. Involving users in development improves communication and results in software that meets needs and requirements better. Gradual developments reduces the impact of training and delivery. It also give you a chance to mould more realistic expectations about what's going to be delivered.'

'What you say makes some sense', she said grudgingly. 'I'd still like to know how do you know when to stop developing the prototype though?'

'Most people are reasonable, Alice, if they get half a chance to be. Demands for change settle down after two or three revisions, if the prototyper is getting users to contribute and is listening to them. Once people see their suggestions taking form in the programs they use, a sense of ownership develops. Once you've got that, most of your user problems are over.'

'That seemed to have happened with the ordering system, all right', agreed Alice. 'But how did you know whether Harry was working or not?' she asked. 'I've never been completely sure about him. A manager has to make sure that staff are doing what they're supposed to be doing, when they're supposed to be doing it.'

'First of all, I had to assume that Harry was technically competent', I said. 'He confirmed that right away by producing some software that did the job. I could see it and use it. I didn't have to be technical to see that it worked.'

'Yes,' she said, 'I guess with your way you do get a chance to see who's bluffing right at the start.'

'Uh-huh', I said. 'Second, my big worry about Harry was his attitude towards the users. I had a bit of a heart-to-heart session with him the first day. Then, I made sure I was at his early sessions with the users. That also gave me a chance to evaluate progress in terms of what was actually finished, instead of what he said was finished or almost finished.'

Alice rolled her eyes. 'Instead of the famous "It's 98 per cent done", you mean?' she groaned.

'Too right', I laughed in agreement. 'Towards the end, I was always there when the system was being shown to Albert and his managers. Those meetings had to be pretty formal and I wasn't sure if Harry was up to that.'

'So you're saying that the development manager really has to be a part of the prototyping process', she mused.

'Yes, every bit of the way', I replied. 'All management should be involved in some demonstrations. Not necessarily at the lowest level, but involved at points where they can contribute to the actual software. For example, it was Albert who suggested adding information to the order form to permit most of his monthly report to be generated from the system.'

'Oh, yes, Albert's been singing your praises loudly enough. But I heard that the ordering department raised a big stink about the extra work of filling out orders after that', said Alice with satisfaction. 'Harry wasn't too delighted about the extra programming work involved, either.'

'Yes, but when it was explained to the ordering people, they accepted it. Especially when they realized it improved their job security and made Albert more aware of the value of their work', I said. 'The software changes Harry had to make were fairly major, but they were easy enough with the fourth-generation language you selected. I think he was mainly getting tired of the project and just blowing off a bit of steam.'

'Was that when he took a couple of unscheduled days off?' asked Alice. 'I'd have done my nut if he'd been working for me then.'

'Well, it was unexpected', I said. 'But the ordering department agreed to work with the system as it was for a week and make a list of problems and suggestions. I suggested that Harry take a few days off in celebration. It's smart not to push too hard all the time.'

'Hmmm,' said Alice. 'Do you really think Harry's up to it? I think I'd like to manage him through the next stage of the development.'

'Oh yes,' I said. 'I think Harry's a bit of a "rough diamond". He can do the programming and he seems to want to please the users. His self-control under fire isn't all that good, but at least he just clams up rather than blows up. Competent programmers who want to please the users and good management to keep them on track are just about all you need.'

'Well,' said Alice. 'There is such a thing as going too far, though. I'm afraid Harry's done that.'

'What do you mean?' I asked, fearing the worst.

'Haven't you heard?' asked Alice. I shook my head. 'He and Ellen got married last week!'

Part 7

'I am very happy to report,' said Alice warmly. 'That my department's experiment with prototyping has proven highly successful. Development of the order system went smoothly throughout and costs were 18.5 per cent lower than budgeted. User polls have shown that confidence in the development function is 32.2 per cent higher than at the beginning of the development. The system has been installed with a minimum amount of disruption to Albert's department. Maintenance demand for the system has been unusually low, 15 per cent below normal.'

Albert broke in. 'Well, it hasn't been too bad, I'll have to say that', he conceded. 'There's still a few more things we need, but it hasn't been all that bad. So far', he growled.

'Those are enhancements, Albert', said Alice with a steely tone. 'We agreed on a moratorium until the users had gained sufficient experience to judge what they really needed next.'

'I know, I know', Albert said. 'I was just pulling your chain a bit. At least for once, I can see I'm getting my money's worth while I'm spending it. And I got to have some fun too, pushing your programmers around, instead of the other way.'

'I wish we'd been able to get exactly what we wanted with those finance packages from Megalith', grumbled Fred. 'They don't really meet my needs for financial creativity.' John gave him a worried look.

'You've always had your money's worth from computing, Albert', said Alice coldly, ignoring Fred. 'I am not convinced yet that prototyping is appropriate in all developments. We will, however, continue to evaluate this approach and employ it where it seems appropriate. If it doesn't work, we'll abandon it. Fortunately, there will be no adverse cost effects if we have to.'

'Well, I don't give a hoot about this prototyping thing you keep going on about, but I'll tell you this,' said Albert, 'I want you to put that new ordering system into the subsidiaries. And I want some say in it like I got this time too.'

'I was planning to anyway', said Alice. 'Prototyping's an ideal way to overcome the language problems with those sites. It will cost more to have our developers on those sites, of course, but it's a lot cheaper than ending up with software they can't use.'

John broke in. 'Well then, I'm glad it's all turned out so well. I certainly think that the order reports that Alice did for Albert have really improved the ways we can do business. I feel like I know what's going on around here a lot better now.' He beamed at everyone. 'You know, we could be doing a lot more of this kind of thing', he said. 'I have this neighbour who works in computers. She says that all this programming stuff is old fashioned now. Her company is involved with these totally amazing things called neurotic networks and . . .'

Discussion

The narrator was able to do almost everything right on this project. He was able to perform a computing service overview of the business first. This allowed him to get to know the business better and to select a useful project of a reasonable size. He let the first meeting with Alice get out of hand a bit, but Alice was a pretty tough opponent and was playing on home ground. The narrator managed to keep the discussion fairly non-technical and not too heated on his part.

The narrator had some real luck in his development staff. Harry, initially highly unpromising, just happened to have pretty much the 'right stuff' for prototyping. I suspect, though, that his conversion was a bit too easy for the narrator. Sue's reactions were typical of disgruntled and fearful users. Like Ellen most users have respect for genuine technical skill when it is being used to their advantage; most people like to be helpful too. Marriage is not normally to be expected from prototyping, however.

The narrator obviously spent some time with Albert during the development. This paid off handsomely. There is no indication if he made sure that John and Fred knew how things were going. If he did not, he should have. His private approach to make peace with Alice was well timed and low key. The narrator let Alice claim all the credit for the success of the prototype. This is the most successful type of technology transfer.

References

Arthur Andersen & Co. (1986) *Trends in Information Technology: 1986*, Chicago.

Avison, D. E. and G. Fitzgerald (1988) 'Information systems development: current themes and future directions', *Information and Software Technology*, October, pp. 458–66.

Baber, R. L. (1989) ' "Software engineering" vs. software engineering'. *Computer*, May, p. 81.

Barron, I. and R. Curnow (1979) *The Future with Microelectronics*, Pinter, London.

Bates, P. E. (1989) 'Prototyping: a motivation', in Shepperd (1989), pp. 1–19.

Bell, C. G., J. C. Mudge, and J. E. McNamara (eds) (1978) *Computer Engineering*, Digital Press, Bedford, Mass.

Bessant, J. R. and K. E. Dickson (1982) *Issues in the Adoption of Microelectronics*, Pinter, London.

Birtwistle, G. M., O.-J. Dahl, B. Myhrhaug, and K. Nygaard (1980) *SIMULA BEGIN*, Chartwell-Bratt, Bromley, Kent.

Bloor, R. (1989) 'How well do "real world" statistics measure up?', *DEC User*, August, pp. 25–8.

Boar, B. H. (1984) *Application Prototyping: A Requirements Definition Strategy for the 80s*, Wiley, New York.

Boehm, B. W. (1981) *Software Engineering Economics*, Prentice Hall, Englewood Cliffs, NJ.

Boehm, B. W. (1987) 'Improving software productivity', *Computer*, September pp. 43–57.

Boehm, B. W. and P. N. Papaccio (1988) 'Understanding and controlling software costs', *IEEE Transactions on Software Engineering*, October, pp. 1462–77.

Boehm, B. W., T. E. Gray, and T. Seewaldt (1984) 'Prototyping versus specifying: a multiproject experiment', *IEEE Transactions on Software Engineering*, May, pp. 290–303.

Bourne, S. R. (1978) 'The UNIX shell', *Bell System Technical Journal*, July–August, pp. 1971–90.

Brender, R. F. (1978) 'Turning cousins into sisters: an example of software smoothing of hardware differences', in Bell *et al.* (1978) pp. 365–78.

Budde, R. (1984) 'Summary of the working group "Very high level languages for prototyping" ', in Budde *et al.* (1984) pp. 393–7.

Budde, R., K. Kuhlenkamp, L. Mathiassen, and H. Zullighoven (eds) (1984). *Approaches to Prototyping*, Springer-Verlag, Berlin.

Budgen, D. (1984) 'The use of prototyping in the design of large concurrent systems', in Budde *et al.* (1984) pp. 49–57.

Butler Cox (1988) *Computer-aided Software Engineering (CASE)*. *Research Report 67*, Butler Cox & Partners, London.

Cole, E. (1989) 'dBASE IV is a godsend—to the competition', *Business Week*, 13 November, p. 79.

Coplin, J., S. Bond, D. Collens, J. Connell, C. A. R. Hoare, G. W. Holmes, P. Ost, D. Robson, M. F. Smith, J. Whalley, C. Whitby-Strevens, and R. W. Witty (1986) *Software: A Vital Key to UK Competitiveness*, Cabinet Office Advisory Council for Applied Research and Development, HMSO, London.

Couger, J. D. and R. A. Zawacki (1980) *Motivating and Managing Computer Personnel*, Wiley, New York.

Dahl, O.-J., E. W. Dijkstra, and C. A. R. Hoare (1972) *Structured Programming*, Academic Press, New York.

Date, C. J. (1977) *An Introduction to Database Systems*, Addison-Wesley, Reading, Mass.

Dearnley, P. A. and P. J. Mayhew, (1984) 'On the use of software development tools in the construction of data processing system prototypes', in Budde *et al.* (1984) pp. 68–79.

Falk, H. (1989) 'Software vendors serve up varied palette for CASE users', *Computer Design*, 1 January, pp. 70–80.

Fischer, G. (1989) 'Human–computer interaction software: lessons learned, challenges ahead', *IEEE Software*, January, pp. 44–52.

Floyd, C. (1984) 'A systematic look at prototyping', in Budde *et al.* (1984) pp. 1–18.

Galitz, W. O. (1980) *Human Factors in Office Automation*, Life Office Management Association, Atlanta, Ga.

Gibson, C. F. and R. L. Nolan, (1974) 'Managing the four stages of EDP growth', *Harvard Business Review*, January–February, pp. 76–88.

Gilb, T. (1976) *Software Metrics*, Chartwell-Bratt, Bromley, Kent.

Graham, D. R. (1989) 'Incremental development: review of nonmonolithic life-cycle development models', *Information and Software Technology*, **31**, no. 1, January/February, pp. 7–20.

Green, T. R. G., S. J. Payne, and G. C. van der Veer (eds) (1983) *The Psychology of Computer Use*, Academic Press, London.

Gries, D. (1971) *Compiler Construction for Digital Computers*, Wiley, New York.

Guest, D. (1989) 'Quality: myths and legends', *Computer Systems Europe*, January, pp. 12–15.

Hammonds, K. H. (1989) 'The spreadsheet that nearly wore Lotus out', *Business Week*, 3 July, pp. 50–2.

Haughton, H. (1989) 'Developing communication protocols—a prototypical approach', in Shepperd (1989) pp. 64–78.

Heckel, P. (1984) *The Elements of Friendly Software Design*, Warner, New York.

Hekmatpour, S. and D. C. Ince (1986) *Rapid Software Prototyping*, Open University, Milton Keynes.

Hirschheim, R. A., (1985) *Office Automation*, Addison-Wesley, Wokingham.

Hix, D. (1989) 'User interfaces: opening a window on the computer', *IEEE Software*, January, pp. 8–10.

Hollinde, I. and K. H. Wagner (1984) 'Experience of prototyping in command and control information systems', in Budde *et al.* (1984) pp. 80–91.

Hollingdale, S. H. and G. C. Tootill (1965) *Electronic Computers*, Penguin Books, Harmondsworth.

Iivari, J. (1984) 'Prototyping in the context of information systems design', in Budde *et al.* (1984) pp. 261–77.

Ince, D. (1987) 'Model answers', *Infomatics*, September, pp. 61–2.

Ince, D. (1988) *Software Development: Fashioning the Baroque*, Oxford University Press, Oxford.

Ince, D. (1989) 'The software prototype', *EXE Magazine*, September, pp. 42–7.

IT-STARTS (1989a) *Developers' Guide*. National Computing Centre, Manchester.

IT-STARTS (1989b) *Developing Systems Together—A Handbook for Users*, National Computing Centre, Manchester.

Jones, C. (1986) *Programming Productivity*, McGraw-Hill, New York.

Jones, R. (1988) 'Breaking into the boardroom', *Infomatics*, September, pp. 55–8.

Jordan, P. W., K. S. Keller, R. W. Tucker, and D. Vogel (1989) 'Software storming: combining rapid prototyping and knowledge engineering', *Computer*, May, pp. 39–48.

Jorgensen, A. H. (1984) 'On the psychology of prototyping', in Budde *et al.* (1984) pp. 278–289.

Kammersgaard, J. and N. Munkegade (1984) 'A discussion of prototyping within a conceptual framework', in Budde *et al.* (1984) pp. 294–321.

Kernighan, B. W. and D. M. Ritchie (1978) *The C Programming Language*, Prentice Hall, Englewood Cliffs, NJ.

Kidder, T. (1981) *The Soul of a New Machine*. Little, Brown, Boston, Mass.

King, J. L. (1983) 'Centralized versus decentralized computing: organisational considerations and management options', *Computing Surveys*, December, pp. 319–49.

King, J. L. and E. L. Schrems (1978) 'Cost–benefit analysis in information systems development and operations', *Computing Surveys*, March, pp. 19–34.

King, J. L. and K. L. Kraemer (1984) 'Evolution and organisational information systems: an assessment of Nolan's stage model', *Communications of the ACM*, May, pp. 466–75.

Kohoutek, H. J. (1984) 'Quality issues in new generation computing', *Proceedings of the International Conference on Fifth Generation Computer Systems*, pp. 695–702.

Kopetz, H. (1979) *Software Reliability*, Macmillan, London.

Kreplin, K.-D. (1984) 'Summary of the working group "Prototyping and database design" ', in Budde *et al* (1984) pp. 177–8.

Lamersdorf, W. and J. W. Schmidt (1984) 'Specification and prototyping of data model semantics', in Budde *et al* (1984) pp. 214–31.

Law, D. (1985) *Prototyping: A State of the Art Report*, National Computing Centre, Manchester.

Lee, B. (1979) *Introducing Systems Analysis and Design*, National Computing Centre, Manchester.

Leibrandt, U. and P. Schnupp (1984) 'An evaluation of PROLOG as a prototyping system', in Budde *et al* (1984) pp. 424–33.

Livesey, P. B. (1984) 'Experience with prototyping in a multi national organisation', in Budde *et al* (1984) p. 92-104.

Lockett, M. (1986) *The Use of Personal Computers by Managers and Professional Staff*, Oxford Institute of Information Management, Templeton College, Oxford.

Loftus, G. R. and E. F. Loftus (1983) *Mind at Play*, Basic Books, New York.

IEEE Scientific Supercomputer Subcommittee (1989) 'The computer spectrum: a perspective on the evolution of computing', *Computer*, November, pp. 57–62.

Luqi (1988) 'Software evolution through rapid prototyping', *Computer*, May, pp. 13–25.

Luqi and V. Berzins (1988) 'Rapidly prototyping real-time systems', *IEEE Software*, September, pp. 25–36.

Luqi and M. Ketabchi (1988) 'A computer-aided prototyping system', *IEEE Software*, March, pp. 66–72.

McCracken, D. D. and M. A. Jackson (1982) 'Life-cycle concept considered harmful', ACM SIGSOFT: Software Engineering Notes, 7, no. 2, April, pp. 29–32.

Martin, J. (1984) *An Information Systems Manifesto*, Prentice Hall, Englewood Cliffs, NJ.

Martin, J. and E. A. Hershey, III (1984) *Information Engineering: A Management White Paper*. KnowledgeWare, Ann Arbor, Mich.

Mason, R. E. A. and T. T. Carey (1983) 'Prototyping interactive information systems', *Communications of the ACM*, May, pp. 347–54.

Mathiassen, L. (1984) 'Summary of the working group "Systems development and prototyping" ', in Budde *et al.* (1984) pp. 255–60.

Maxwell, P. (1988) 'C++ for application design', *Systems International*, November, pp. 79–80.

Mayhew, P. J., C. J. Worsley and P. A. Dearnley (1989) 'Controlling the software prototyping process: a change classification approach', in Shepperd (1989), pp. 36–59.

Metzger, P. W. (1981) *Managing a Programming Project*, 2nd edn, Prentice Hall, Englewood Cliffs, N.J.

Monckemeyer, M. and T. Spitta (1984) 'Concept and experiences of prototyping in a software-engineering-environment with NATURAL', in Budde *et al.* (1984) pp. 122–35.

Myers, B. A. (1989) 'User-interface tools: introduction and survey', *IEEE Software*, January, pp. 15–23.

Myers, W. (1989) 'Allow plenty of time for large-scale software', *IEEE Software*, July, pp. 92–9.

Newman, I. (1989) 'Interfaces for applications portability', *Telecommunications*, April, pp. 56–60.

Nolan, R. L. (1979) 'Managing the crises in data processing', *Harvard Business Review*, March–April, pp. 115–26.

Nosek, J. T. (1984) 'Organization design choices to facilitate evolutionary development of prototype information systems', in Budde *et al.* (1984) pp. 341–55.

Nulty, P. (1989) 'America's toughest bosses', *Fortune*, 27 February, pp. 24–30.

ORACLE (1985) *Pro*C User's Guide*, Oracle Corporation, Belmont, Calif.

ORACLE (1986) *SQL*Forms Designer's Reference*, Version 2.0, Oracle Corporation, Belmont, Calif.

Parbst, F. (1984) 'Experience with prototyping in an IBM-based installation', in Budde *et al.* (1984) pp. 152–64.

Perelman, Ch. and L. Olbrechts-Tyteca (1969) *The New Rhetoric: A Treatise on Argumentation*, trans. J. Wilkinson and P. Weaver, University of Notre Dame Press, Notre Dame, Ind.

Porter, M. E. and V. E. Millar (1985) 'How information gives you competitive advantage', *Harvard Business Review*, July–August, pp. 149–60.

Powell, M. S. (1987) 'Strongly typed user interfaces in an abstract data store', *Software Practice and Experience*, April, pp. 241–66.

Raghavan, S. A. and D. R. Chand (1989) 'Diffusing software-engineering methods', *IEEE Software*, July, pp. 81–90.

Pratt, T. W. (1975) *Programming Languages: Design and Implementation*, Prentice Hall, Englewood Cliffs, NJ.

Riddle W. E. (1984) 'Advancing the state of the art in software system prototyping', in Budde *et al* (1984) pp. 19–30.

Rzevski, G. (1984) 'Prototypes versus pilot systems: strategies for evolutionary information system development', in Budde *et al* (1984) pp. 256–367.

Salter, T. (1989) 'Management information prototyping', in Shepperd (1989) pp. 20–35.

Samish, F. (1989) 'Are they biting?', *Multi-User Computing*, January, pp. 27–9.

Scanlon, D. A. (1989) 'Structured flowcharts outperform pseudocode: an experimental comparison', *IEEE Software*, September, pp. 28–36.

Schnupp, P. (1984) 'Comments on "The ADA/ED system: a large-scale experiment in software prototyping using SETL" ', in Budde *et al* (1984) pp. 418–23.

Scown, S. J. (1985) *The Artificial Intelligence Experience: An Introduction*, Digital Equipment Corporation, Maynard, Mass.

Sengler, H. E. (1983) 'A model of the understanding of a program and its impact on the design of the programming language GRADE', in Green *et al.* (1983) pp. 91–106.

Shandle, J. (1989) 'It's time to grow up', *Electronics*, June, pp. 74–5.

Shepperd, M. J. (ed.) (1989) *Rapid Prototyping for the Software Developer*, Wolverhampton Polytechnic.

Smith, M. F. (1981) 'Field prototyping for software—a practical approach to implementation', *Microprocessors and Microsystems*, January–February, pp. 29–30.

Smith, M. F. (1986) 'A taxonomic classification of dedicated microprocessor applications', *Journal of Microcomputer Applications*, **9**, pp. 63–81.

Smith, M. F. and J.-M. Lador (1984) 'Selection of a standard programming language for an oil service consultancy', *Computers and Geosciences*, **10**, nos 2–3, pp. 311–15.

Smith, M. F., Y. Hoffner and M. A. Sealey (1985) 'Mapping high-level syntax and structure into assembly language', *IEEE Micro*, August, pp. 67–81.

Snow, C. P. (1964) *The Two Cultures: And a Second Look*, Cambridge University Press, Cambridge.

Stackpole (1962) *The Air Officer's Guide*, Stackpole, Harrisburg, Pa.

STARTS (1987) *The STARTS Guide*, National Computing Centre, Manchester.

Stroustrup, B. (1986) *The C++ Programming Language*, Addison-Wesley, Reading, Mass.

Sykes, J. B. (1976) *The Concise Oxford Dictionary of Current English*, Oxford University Press, Oxford.

Talbot, D. and R. W. Witty (1983) 'Software Engineering Strategy', Alvey Programme, London.

Tanik, M. M. and R. T. Yeh (1989) 'Rapid prototyping in software development', *Computer*, May, pp. 9–10.

Tavolato, P. and K. Vincena (1984) 'A prototyping methodology and its tool', in Budde *et al.* (1984) pp. 434–46.

Thomas, J. C. and W. A. Kellogg (1989) 'Minimizing ecological gaps in interface design', *IEEE Software*, January, pp. 78–86.

Tingley, G. A. (1984) 'Comments on "On the psychology of prototyping" by

Anker Helms Jorgensen', in Budde *et al.* (1984) pp. 292-3.

Tufte, E. R. (1983) *The Visual Display of Quantitative Information*, Graphics Press, Cheshire, Conn.

Webster, D. E. (1988) 'Mapping the design information representation terrain', *Computer*, December, pp. 8-23.

Weinberg, G. M. (1971) *The Psychology of Computer Programming*, Van Nostrand-Reinhold, New York.

Yourdon, E. (1989) *Modern Structured Analysis*, Prentice Hall, Englewood Cliffs, NJ.

Zortech (1986) *Zortech C++ Compiler*, Zortech, Arlington, Mass.

Zortech (1987) *Zortech C++ Tools*, Zortech, Arlington, Mass.

Index

Analysis, 26–27, 61, 65, 104, 121, 124
Analysts (*see* Programmers and analysts)
Artificial intelligence (AI), 74, 150
  LISP, 150
  PROLOG, 150
  expert systems, 150, 166
Analytical development methods (*see* Traditional development methods)

Blueprint (*see* Traditional development methods)
Business requirements, 18, 39, 95–96, 108, 112, 117–118, 123–124, 131–132

CASE (*see* Computer aided software engineering)
Charging (*see* Contracts)
Communication, 17, 53, 64, 83–84, 88
Computer aided design (CAD), 74, 148, 150
Computer aided software engineering (CASE), 74–76
  problems of, 76
Computer illiteracy, 18, 39, 93–94
Contracts, 38, 74–75, 125–126
Costs, 37–39, 64, 66, 75–76, 84, 96–97, 104–106, 113, 121, 123, 125–126, 140, 142, 144, 153
Creativity, 26–27, 34

Custom software, 2, 7–8, 35–36, 38, 41, 155

Data,
  requirements, 42, 137, 160, 171, 172
  database and prototyping, 99, 119–120, 129–130, 136–138
  (*see also* Database management systems)
Database management systems (DBMS), 66, 144, 147, 149, 151, 155, 159–160, 169
  Datatrieve, 144
  dBase, 7, 144
  Informix, 144
  Oracle, 144–147
  Ashton-Tate, 7
  HCI, 145–146
Defence, Ministry of (UK), 74
Defense, Department of (US), 2, 69, 74
Delivery, 14, 18, 57–58, 62–64, 95, 98–99, 112, 119–121, 124, 132–136, 139–140, 144
Design, 17, 43–44, 56, 59, 61–62, 69, 114, 137
Dialectic of proof, 14–16
Documentation, 2, 55, 63–64, 73–74, 100, 120, 132–133

Education/training, 17–18, 30, 54, 73, 93–94, 113–114, 124, 133, 152, 154
Error, 17–18, 24, 40, 100, 127–128, 152

Estimation, 14–15, 103–109
Expectations, 35, 54, 79

Failure, of software, 7, 13, 16–18, 22–23,
    25, 36, 38–41, 110, 112, 115–116
Familiarization, 19, 90, 152
Feasibility, 61, 62
Formal methods (*see* Languages, very
    high level)
Function (functionality), 36, 38, 42–44,
    56, 63, 97, 107–108, 120, 123–124,
    126, 131, 139, 142

Graphical-user interface (GUI) (*see*
    Human computer interface)

Hardware, 2, 18, 22–23, 58, 65, 124, 169
    personal computers (PCs), 16, 18–20
Human computer interface (HCI), 44,
    141, 143, 145–146, 152–155
    costs, 152
Human factors, 26, 33–34, 120–122,
    160–161

Integration, 56, 114, 129–130, 134
Interfaces, 85, 114, 125, 129
Implementation, 62

Languages, fourth generation (4GL),
    66, 147, 151, 178
Languages, third generation (3GL):
    ADA, 140, 149
    ALGOL, 23
    APL, 142
    BASIC, 140, 142–143
    C, 140–141, 142–143, 146–147
    C++, 149
    COBOL, 23, 140
    FORTRAN, 23, 59
    Object-oriented languages (OOL),
        149–150
    PASCAL, 140
    PL/, 140
    SIMULA, 149
Languages, very high level (VHLL):
    ADS, 148
    executable specification, 149
    HOS, 76, 149
    OBJ, 76
    VDM, 76, 149
    Z, 76

Management, 7, 17, 92–93, 63–64
    issues, 112–122
    leadership, 109–110
    manageability, 70
    prototyping benefits, 84
    prototyping management, 48–49, 103–
        111, 112–122
    software managers, 31, 90–91. 112–
        114
Maintenance, 18, 54, 57, 63, 65, 75–76,
    95, 99–100, 124, 133
    critical mass, 3, 40
    maintainability, 40, 70, 95
    prototype, 135–136
Man–machine interface (MMI) (*see*
    Human-computer interface)
Methodologies, 48, 71–73
    automation of, 74
    costs of, 73
    formal methods (*see* Languages, very
        high level
Metrics, 14–15, 69, 121–122, 189

Office automation (OA), 16, 19, 150
Organization, 17–18, 25, 42, 58, 60, 114,
    117–118, 131, 158

Performance, 37, 42–43, 75–76, 98–99,
    124, 134, 142, 147, 153
Phase-out, 63
Planning, 123–125, 130–131
Prediction (*see* Estimation)
Productivity, 2, 69–70, 72, 84, 121, 149
Programmers and analysts, 27–31, 75,
    88, 90, 94
Proof, 14–16, 157
    dialectic of, 14–16 (*see also* Dialectic
        of proof)
    scientific, 14–15
Prototyping:
    adoption of, 57–59
    benefits of, 53–55, 82
    breadboard, 43
    cost factor, 59
    definitions, 44–45
    deliverables, 119–121, 131–136
    design, 43
    evaluation, 82
    evolutionary, 5, 44, 49–50, 59–60, 85–
        86, 124, 134–136, 158–159
    features, 4–5
    incremental development, 44

implementation, 126–136
large-scale, 128–131, 160
life cycles, 123–128
limited application, 58–59
manager, 48–49, 103–111, 112–122
mock-up, 44
model, 44
problems, 55–57, 127
rapid prototyping (*see* Rapid
 development)
scope, 47–48
simulation, 44
skeleton, 44
strategies, 45–47
testing and evaluation, 44
throw-away, 44, 49–50, 59, 124, 134–
 136, 158–159
tools, 4, 79, 83, 86, 100, 121, 139–151,
 159–160
user development, 45
Psychological factors, 20, 28–29, 54, 58,
 67, 88, 90–91, 121–122, 153–154

Quality, 2, 24, 41, 54, 70, 72, 107, 112,
 118–119, 121, 132

Rapid development, 46–47, 95, 97–98,
 127, 139
Requirements, 2, 69, 71, 76, 152

Skills, 17–18, 39, 57–58, 60, 65–66, 79,
 88–90, 94, 126, 153
Software
 complexity, 16, 56, 58, 69
 correctness, 70
 costs, 37
 custom (*see* Custom software)
 development approaches, 3
 (*see also* Traditional development
  approaches; Software
  engineering)
 developer (see Programmers and
  analysts)
 embedded, 23–24
 external, 37–38, 57, 121
 fitness for use, 70
 maintenance (*see* Maintenance)

life cycle, 62, 123–128
metrics, 69, 83, 121–122
packaged, 23–24, 121
portability (*see* Software reuse)
problems, 16–18
productivity (*see* Productivity)
quality (*see* Quality)
reliability, 70
reuse, 69, 98–99, 153
size, 69, 98–99
(*see also* Success of software; Failure of
 software)
Software engineering, 3–4, 45, 51, 54,
 68–77, 160–161, 177–179
 problems, 73–74
 prototyping, 77, 134, 157
Spreadsheets, 7, 21, 147–148, 154–155
 Lotus, 7, 147, 154–155
Staff issues, 75, 89, 91, 107, 113, 126, 160
Standards, 76, 96, 112, 118–119, 140, 147
Structured methodologies (*see*
 Methodologies)
Success of software, 7, 13, 16, 20–24,
 115–116, 120

Technology transfer, 79, 82–86, 95–100
 prototyping evaluation, 82
 costs, 96–97
Testing, 44, 54, 56, 64, 73, 99, 115, 134
Traditional development approach, 61–
 64, 66
Translation, 56, 134–135
Training (*see* Education/training)

Users, 32–33, 34, 39, 45, 53–54, 57, 63–
 64, 89, 91–92, 114–115, 126–128,
 152–153
 development, 45
 problems, 32–33
 prototyping, 54, 87–94, 126–128
 testing, 121–122
 types, 32
UNIX, 19, 141, 143–144

Word processing (*see* Office
 automation)